GOING THE
EXTRA
MILE

GOING THE
EXTRA
MILE

THE "DO IT NOW" PRINCIPLE

JUDITH WILLIAMSON

MEDIA

Published 2022 by Gildan Media LLC
aka G&D Media
www.GandDmedia.com

FIRST EDITION 2022

Front cover design by David Rheinhardt of Pyrographx

Interior design by Meghan Day Healey of Story Horse, LLC

Library of Congress Cataloging-in-Publication Data is available upon request

ISBN: 978-1-7225-0595-0

10   9   8   7   6   5   4   3   2   1

Contents

Going the Extra Mile

1. The Do It Now Principle

In planning to acquire your share of the riches,
let no one influence you to scorn the dreamer.
—NAPOLEON HILL

Dreams are today's answers to tomorrow's questions.
—EDGAR CAYCE

2. The Little Things of Living

It is a curious fact that most people will do something to help
humanity, even when they wouldn't do it just to help you.
—NAPOLEON HILL

If you want to lift yourself up, lift someone else up.
—BOOKER T. WASHINGTON

3. The Service Essentials

The place to begin is in your own mind.
Your success and failure are in your own mind.
—Napoleon Hill

I believe that if one always looked at the skies,
one would end up with wings.
—Gustave Flaubert

4. The Spirit of Service

When you have talked yourself into what you want,
right there is the place to stop talking and begin
saying it with deeds.
—Napoleon Hill

The question isn't who is going to let me;
it's who is going to stop me.
—Ayn Rand

5. The Channel of Giving

Giving is a form of expression and giving is living.
—Napoleon Hill

Light tomorrow with today.
—Elizabeth Barrett Browning

6. The Companions on the Journey

A kindly word here, a kindly deed there,
a pleasant smile everywhere, and this world
would be a better place for all mankind.
—NAPOLEON HILL

It's time to start living the life you've imagined.
—HENRY JAMES

7. The Discovery of Mission

The principle of Going the Extra Mile is the
master strategy of the entire philosophy, for it
gets action. It is the active principle.
—NAPOLEON HILL

A dream doesn't become reality through magic,
it takes sweat, determination and hard work.
—COLIN POWELL

8. The Purpose of Work

You know, work is a liaison office between
our desires and their fulfillment.
—NAPOLEON HILL

The only person you are destined to become
is the person you decide to be.
—RALPH WALDO EMERSON

9. The "To Do" List that Matters

A little job well done is the first step towards a bigger one.
—NAPOLEON HILL

Strive not to be a success but rather to be of value.
—ALBERT EINSTEIN

10. The Compensation of Giving

Get into the habit of Going the Extra Mile
because of the pleasure you get out of it,
and because of what it does to you.
—NAPOLEON HILL

We cannot hold a torch to light another's
path without brightening our own.
—BEN SWEETLAND

11. The Habit of Gratitude

Don't forget to express gratitude daily,
by prayer and affirmation,
for the blessings you have.
—NAPOLEON HILL

Do small things with great love.
—MOTHER TERESA

12. The Alchemy of Prosperity

*The river is the brain. The flowing force is the
power of thought. The failure side of the stream is
negative thought; the success side is positive thought.*
—Napoleon Hill

*Hang on to your hat. Hang on to your hope.
And wind the clock, for tomorrow is another day.*
—E.B. White

13. The Plus Factor

*Cosmic habitforce will take over this habit of
Going the Extra Mile and make it a fixation
which will be of untold benefit to you. You'll find
yourself doing it automatically, just for the
good feeling it gives you deep down inside.*
—Napoleon Hill

Boldness has genius, power, and magic in it.
—Johann Wolfgang von Goethe

Foreword

Napoleon Hill spent his life developing a success philosophy that would help anyone achieve success. Hill often emphasized the importance of the principle of "Going the Extra Mile" in order to achieve success.

Going the Extra Mile simply means that you render more service at your job than you are being paid for. You also must do it with a positive mental attitude. Napoleon Hill said that Going the Extra Mile was not an idea developed by man. Instead, it was part of nature's handiwork, like when a single kernel of corn produces multiple ears at harvest time.

Man may ignore the principle of Going the Extra Mile, but he cannot do so and enjoy the fruits of lasting success.

Napoleon Hill often wrote about the benefits of Going the Extra Mile and used stories to illustrate his point. One story he told was about an elderly woman who stepped into a department store to escape the rain. The salesmen in the store knew the woman wasn't likely to purchase anything, so they all ignored her—all but one young man. This young man offered the elderly woman a chair so that she could rest her feet. The rain eventually stopped and the woman left the store. A few weeks later the department store received a phone call from the woman; she was furnishing a mansion in Scotland and wanted to work directly with the young man who had assisted her on that rainy day. The woman was Andrew Carnegie's mother and she wanted the young man to help her at Skibo Castle in Scotland.

Another great example of Going the Extra Mile involves William C. Durant, founder of General Motors. One Saturday, Durant stopped at a bank and discovered that it was closed. A young bank teller, Carroll Downes, saw Mr. Durant and went to the door. Mr. Durant explained that he was going out of town on business and needed to cash a check. Carroll Downes told Mr. Durant that while the bank was closed, the vault had not been sealed for the day and the check could still be cashed. Mr. Durant gave Carroll his business card and invited him to stop by his office sometime. Eventually, Carroll Downes began working for Mr. Durant. Carroll continued Going the Extra Mile for Mr. Durant until he was promoted and given over a million dollars in stock options.

As you can see from these stories, it truly pays dividends to go the extra mile. If you are not Going the Extra Mile, I urge you to start today in order to achieve the life of your dreams.

—Don Green
CEO/Executive Director of
the Napoleon Hill Foundation

Introduction

When I was approached to write a self-help book on Napoleon Hill's principle of Going the Extra Mile, I wondered why the world would need another book on a principle so common, so readily understood, so practical, and so simple, that it is written about in the Bible concisely and directly. Jesus states in the Gospels: "Do unto others as you would have others do unto you." If that's not Going the Extra Mile, then I don't know what is.

Who does not understand this commandment? I believe everyone understands the commandment, but the lack is in the application, the *doing* part. When someone gives you a command such as mail the letter, take out the garbage, feed the cat, water the plants, sweep the floor, do the dishes, and wash the car, it is generally understood. But the proof as we know it to be is in the doing. The commandment then becomes a question that asks: Do I do unto others as I would have others do unto me? Probably not.

What holds us back in the doing? In the Bible we are told: "And whosoever shall compel thee to go a mile, go with him twain." It gets even better. Instead of simply doing one thing, we are now told to "go the extra mile" and do two! We may question why someone can't do these things for themselves. Why are we needed to assist and to do what a person is not capable of doing for themselves? Or perhaps, what they choose not to do for themselves. Even worse, they may seek out others to do for themselves what they prefer not to do. In preferring not to do, you can eliminate yourself right out of existence. The basic challenge in this life is to do, to risk, and not to scale back and simply to not opt out.

Why should we contemplate or even plague ourselves with these questions? Getting back to the basic commandment, if we follow the guidelines that are simple and direct we are bound to hit the mark every single time. Questions and concerns aside, in Emerson's words, "Do the thing and you will have the power." To become what you dream about, you must take action and begin. Without a beginning there can be no ending.

So, in making a case for Going the Extra Mile, I have included ideas, exercises, applications, visualizations, and much more to get you started on the right course. It is my assumption that the reader of this book wants more information on Dr. Hill's Principles of Success, but is not a graduate student in the Science of Success curriculum.

Together we are going to build a structure for enriching your life and the lives of others, one success principle at a time—by beginning at the beginning. These building blocks will aid you in determining a positive direction for your life and energizing the power to make it happen. You cannot do this in a day, a week, or even a month. For many it takes a lifetime to fully develop, but without it you will be like a ship without a rudder—tossed aimlessly on stormy seas.

Irish author John O'Donohue states: "Even though your body is always bound to one place, your mind is a relentless voyager. The mind has a magnificent, creative restlessness that always brings it on a new journey. Even in the most sensible and controlled lives there is often an undertow of longing that would deliver them to distant shores. There is something within you that is not content to remain fixed within any one frame." The cure for this longing? Mark Twain advises: "Twenty years from now you will be more disappointed by the things you didn't do than by the ones you did do. So throw off the bowlines. Sail away from the safe harbor. Catch the trade winds in your sails. Explore. Dream. Discover." The obvious answer then is to get moving and to get on with it. That is step one.

For fair winds and following seas in your life (with occasional storms too), Dr. Hill's Philosophy would be a North Star to guide you and set the course of a lifetime.

Begin now by having eyes to envision your course, taking personal initiative in charting your course direction, and persistence in maintaining a steady hand at the wheel. Before taking leave and pulling anchor, design your course of study using this philosophy and you will always arrive at your chosen destination ahead of others.

All that is asked of you is to start right where you are, in this moment, here and now. Follow the directions by first taking action in using the principle of Going the Extra Mile to position yourself on the navigational course of a lifetime—your lifetime.

Time to sail!

Bon Voyage.
—Judy Williamson

Do It Now

A Prelude and Practice Sheet—Start NOW.
1. Say "Thank You"
2. Smile
3. Pick up litter
4. Phone a friend
5. Round up at the cash register
6. Pet an animal
7. Bring a homemade dessert
8. Pray
9. Hold open a door
10. Say "No Charge"
11. Move aside for faster traffic
12. Plant daffodils
13. Feed the birds, squirrels, and outdoor wildlife
14. Donate food, clothes, and books
15. Clean up your mess
16. Listen, not talk

17. Read to a child
18. Say grace
19. Show up!
20. Think with a positive mind set
21. Cancel negative thoughts
22. Go to bed early
23. Praise a friend
24. Compliment a stranger
25. Express gratitude
26. Eat fruits and vegetables
27. Drink enough water daily
28. Be a good-finder
29. Help the homeless
30. Rejoice! Be glad
31. Listen to good music
32. Take a stroll outdoors
33. Photograph a masterpiece of nature
34. Talk to an animal
35. Listen to the birds
36. Praise God
37. Count your blessings
38. Inspire others
39. Refrain from criticism
40. Be the good you want to see in the world

Chapter 1

The Do It Now Principle

In planning to acquire your share of the riches,
let no one influence you to scorn the dreamer.
—NAPOLEON HILL

Welcome to a habit that will absolutely change your life for the better, right now. Beginning this very moment—today—you can immediately prosper and enrich your life from this habit. What is it? It is the gem of all habits: Going the Extra Mile. When you begin to act in accordance with this habit, there will be no returning to the former you. All it takes is to *Do It Now!*

In Napoleon Hill's *Science of Success Course* he states:

> If I had to choose but one of the seventeen principles of success and rest my chances on that principle alone, I would, without hesitation, choose Going the Extra Mile, because this is the principle through which one can make himself indispensable to others.

This declaration alone would cause anyone to listen attentively to what the author has to say and to follow Hill's teachings. Begin here if you want to travel on this proven road to success—the road to enduring riches.

Dr. Hill's illustrious student and partner, W. Clement Stone, states emphatically that the key to success is just to "Do It Now." What, you may ask, is the "do" part of doing it now? Simply, it is the action part of the philosophy that brings you the end result you are seeking. By shifting yourself into action, you are notifying the Universe that you are serious about putting the Laws of Increasing Returns and Compensation in your debt. It may be likened to turning a key in the ignition of a vehicle that starts the driving process, or lighting a fire underneath a pot that starts the cooking process, but regardless the most important part is in the action of beginning.

You may also be asking yourself why Going the Extra Mile is so important to begin with in seeking success. There are numerous reasons to consider. One of the most explicit reasons is that it brings favorable attention to you. A person who consistently goes the extra mile with no expectation of compensation from the recipient creates a Universal ledger in their behalf that sooner or later pays off compound dividends to the person that rendered the service.

You may be skeptical at first, but if you follow the *Do It Now* directive daily you will find that your progression is not sterile and inactive, but rather fertile and growing.

Let's get started by taking a look at why developing the habit of consistently Going the Extra Mile creates an atmosphere of abundance for you and promises to deliver more than you have actually contributed or earned.

Here are some reasons to consider as you take Napoleon Hill's counsel and discern the benefits of cultivating the crowning jewel of all the principles, Going the Extra Mile.

1. As you become the person who goes the extra mile and contributes more than is expected or immediately compensated, the spotlight begins to shine on your performance and others notice something different, something more about the service you render.

2. The Law of Contrast enters the picture as others watch you. Most people do not go the first mile let alone the second mile in making a contribution. When someone is asked to do something extra, the reply most often heard is, "That's not my job." This can be heard daily in work environments, and often becomes a mantra for those who do not excel or succeed beyond their present position.

3. The Laws of Increasing and Decreasing Returns come into play. People willing to go the extra mile are eventually compensated for doing more than they are paid to do because they stand out from the crowd given this one habit. And, because they are

noticed for a willingness to extend themselves and give without the expectation of getting, they are recognized for their ability to make a strong contribution to the job at hand. Decreasing returns are for those individuals who can only do what they are paid to do and nothing more.

4. The person who consistently goes the extra mile makes him or herself indispensable because they can be relied upon to get the job done. Anyone looking for assistance will seek that person out first because of their reputation of being a doer and not a talker. Everyone knows that talk is cheap, and Dr. Hill states that "opinions are the cheapest commodity on Earth because everyone has them." But, an individual stands out from others by taking action and doing something to address whatever needs to be done. Theirs is a course of action, not talk.

5. As a person Going the Extra Mile, you develop your success skillset; you learn more and become able to address multiple tasks because you have taken personal initiative in learning how to do things. Therefore, for someone seeking help, you are the one who offers the needed service.

6. By assuming responsibility that you are not told to take, you move up the success ladder because this one single habit makes you stand out from the crowd. It gives a person the subtle edge that makes the critical difference in being given the next opportunity or not.

7. Consistently Going the Extra Mile makes you a candidate for promotion because others do not follow this habit and therefore are not eligible for more responsibilities related to supervision and leadership. They are already being compensated for what they are worth.

8. Most importantly this habit of Going the Extra Mile allows a person the flexibility in seeking and procuring employment from various organizations that value this type of personal initiative at salaries of a person's own choosing.

9. You might consider the Going the Extra Mile (GEM) habit common sense, but it is well known that common sense is not very common at all. Instead the habit of Going the Extra Mile might be termed supernatural common sense since it divinely inspires the practitioner developing this habit to call on the Universe for promised compensation—and to even expect it.

10. By utilizing this one principle, you can take the results to the bank metaphorically and physically because it does work in your behalf every single time you use it.

The above characteristics are powerful reasons for putting Going the Extra Mile into practice. It is the easiest principle to get started with because it requires nothing additional except added effort on your part. Without effort or action, nothing moves and neither do you. In fact you regress, because you may think that you are maintaining your positive foothold but you are slipping backwards.

Others, who are practicing this habit, are bracing for the home stretch. Take a lesson from the Kentucky Derby and just watch what can turn the tide in a race to determine a winner. It is not simply being in the starting line up at the race. It is going the extra measure to win by a nose or a head, not a mile. A little means a lot in Going the Extra Mile. It is the extra edge that determines the winner each and every time.

Now that some of the benefits have been introduced about Going the Extra Mile, it is hoped that your interest is peaked. Still you may be asking, what exactly is it that I *do* and how do I know what that extra effort looks like in the real world? This is a common question and one that should be considered in order for you to make the fastest progress in your effort to set yourself apart from the crowd.

Napoleon Hill often asks us to consider how things work in our everyday world. There can be effort and constructive effort and it is your obligation to know which is which. Given your desire to be of better service than the average person, you need to determine in what direction you want to move.

If you work in an organization and aspire to a higher or better paying position, it is a good idea to learn the type of work that is required and then position yourself to make a contribution to that type of work. By volunteering to go the extra mile without pay you will set yourself apart and be noticed for your characteristics of doing more than you are paid to do.

Just this one trait will enable you to be recognized for your willingness to be of service whenever and wherever that service may be needed. Stories abound about the person who shows up, volunteers, works long hours without pay, and eventually is asked to become an employee or is promoted to a higher paying position. Most biographies tell stories of rough starts that lead to monumental outcomes because a person refused to quit and continued to be willing to help where and when needed without pay.

For example, consider the following questions:

1. Have you ever been asked to stay beyond your working time to complete a project?
2. Have you ever been requested to come in on a day when you were not assigned to work?
3. Have you ever agreed to work without pay in order to assist someone who was ill or needed to be elsewhere?
4. Have you ever contributed to or participated in projects that were not job related, but that the organization was sponsoring?
5. Have you ever gotten up early or stayed late in order to complete something that was needed by a person in management the next day?
6. Have you ever taken responsibility to do something that needed to be done but was not your assigned job?

7. Have you ever offered assistance to someone needing help who could not benefit you directly?

8. Have you ever gone out of your way to be of immediate assistance to someone in need even though it was an inconvenience to you?

9. Have you ever contributed your time or talent to a person below you just to be of assistance?

10. Have you looked for ways to make a difference for someone via lending a hand, completing a project, physically assisting them when needed, being polite, avoiding criticism, and positively commenting on a job they did well?

If you thoughtfully answer the above questions you will come up with several ways of immediately Going the Extra Mile in order to jumpstart your own progression towards success. If you have done some of the things listed above, congratulations. You are on the beam as Dr. Hill would say. If you have not done any or very few of the above, now is the time to consider beginning right where you are to address how and when you can start. Be alert to the opportunities as they come along. Put yourself in the position to be of help, and those who are the recipients of your unexpected service will not forget it.

Other simple and basic ways of getting started are common courtesies that include:

1. Holding the door for someone.

2. Addressing a person by their name and giving them a simple, sincere compliment such as: "I like

the outfit you are wearing today. It makes you look special."

3. Joining someone different for lunch by asking: "May I join you for lunch?"

4. Inquiring about a person's family if they enjoy sharing stories about their home life.

5. Asking about a person's pets and making a positive comment about their unique names.

6. Engaging in a person's interests for a short conversation. What do they enjoy doing outside of work? Do they have a favorite hobby?

7. Offer to be of service by stopping to address a concern such as a low tire, a dead battery, a needed ride home, heavy bags that need to be carried, a helpful, steady hand in climbing the stairs, etc., are all ways of being of immediate service.

8. When you see a need, fill it! Lend a stamp, pick up a dropped item, help locate a missing phone, bring a treat to work, remind a person of a meeting, empty a garbage can, and write a note of thanks.

9. Dr. Hill states that this habit of rendering more service than expected by deliberate intent will cause others to be in competition for your services.

10. Do it now. Go the extra mile. Show gratitude to the people in your life by telling them you appreciate them. Words have power and are action oriented when they are both spoken and written.

11. Abide by the Biblical directive to go the extra mile. In Matthew 5:41 it states: "And if anyone forces you to go one mile, go with him twain."

I hope by now that you are getting the idea of what exactly is meant by Going the Extra Mile. Suffice it to say that when you give, you receive back. Perhaps not in the way you expect, or would like, but nevertheless you are always compensated. When you are alert to the benefits of Going the Extra Mile, you do not hesitate to continue the practice because it benefits you and gives you strength for making a strong personal success foundation.

In Dr. Hill's *Science of Success Philosophy* there are seventeen interconnected principles that operate as a chain joined one link at a time. These principles can act independently, but their strength is in the combined use of the concepts. As you learn and integrate one concept at a time into your lifestyle, you become akin to a spiritual body builder who—through exercise, practice, and repetition—strengthens his body with a vision towards improvement.

Much in the same way you will be strengthening your interior self through assimilation of the core principles of this philosophy. Without the Big Four Principles, the philosophy would fall short of being the integrative, life changing course of instruction that has enabled Dr. Hill's work to stand the test of time. Going the Extra Mile is not only one of the major four principles, but the necessary catalyst for getting the whole thing started and maintaining the necessary traction on your success journey.

Andrew Carnegie, W. Clement Stone, and Napoleon Hill all used the principle of Going the Extra Mile initially in order to jumpstart their success process before they each fully recognized the opportunities that the Universe had in store for them. Activating this one principle prepares the mind to receive the big opportunities as they present themselves.

The other main principles of Definiteness of Purpose, Master Mind Alliance, and Applied Faith all enter the process at the time you are ready to receive and incorporate the information. Once recognized, these four principles work in tandem to enable you to achieve whatever it is that you desire most in life. But without Going the Extra Mile there is no promise of there being a solid foundation upon which to build the other cornerstones to success.

It is important to track your progress in Going the Extra Mile. Too often people consider doing or imagine doing tasks or activities that resemble this principle, but they never get beyond the drawing board. The one necessary ingredient for Going the Extra Mile is action.

Let's say that a holiday has come and you imagine the lovely response you will receive from a special recipient to whom you are going to give a very special gift. You see the gift in your mind's eye. It is wrapped in iridescent blue paper, has an enormous white, sparkling bow, and taped on the top of the box is a silver envelope with a designer card inside containing all your special thoughts for the recipient. Perfect. But, the day arrives, and you have neglected to purchase, wrap, sign and seal the card, and deliver the gift. Do you expect appreciation from the intended recipient? Do you receive a "thank you" card? Do you have a sense of fulfillment in having given the special gift? Of course not. It was only a vivid passing daydream on your part, but never taken out of your imagination into reality. End result. Nothing.

The same occurs with Going the Extra Mile. Only in the doing do you receive results. Not in the imagination or in the contemplation. That is where the *Do It Now!* command comes into play. The smallest least action is worth more than the greatest intention. Remember that. Let me say it again, the smallest least action is worth more than the greatest intention. Hold and remember that thought because it is in doing that we receive. The doer is the hero in the story of success.

Record Keeping Suggestions

So, in order to be accountable, I suggest keeping track in written fashion of your actions taken on a daily basis that record how you are Going the Extra Mile. Do this on large note cards or in a journal. Document what you did. Begin by numbering your actions and then indicating completion by placing a check-mark in front of the number.

For even more accountability and tracking of your Going the Extra Mile performance, I would suggest leaving a space after each item wherein you can note a response to the action taken. This allows you to track not only your accountability in taking action, but also what "results" you received from the action taken. Some actions may show immediate results, others could take much longer—a day, a year, even a lifetime.

This system of accounting is only for you and does not have to be lengthy. It could take fewer than ten minutes in the morning, but it demonstrates that you are taking the principle of Going the Extra Mile seriously while simultaneously putting the Universe in your debt.

If you use a journal, make sure that you create lists and not paragraphs. The revelation that is being sought is that the actions are being completed daily and results are being noted.

Notice that nothing has been said about finances. These actions do not involve money or gift giving. They can even be done anonymously. The point is to put the Universe in your debt and to activate the Laws of Increasing Returns and Compensation. These are natural laws and follow the organization of the Universe.

When a farmer plants a crop, much work is done prior to the harvest. If a good harvest occurs, the reward can be tenfold to a hundredfold. Tilling the soil, planting the seeds, watering the plants, and fertilizing the crops, are all actions taken prior to the harvest. Much time is invested before any return is achieved. The same is true in your life's work.

The purpose of this book is to introduce you to the principle of Going the Extra Mile. Know that knowledge is not enough regarding this principle. Knowledge is the lowest component on the Hierarchy of Educational Objectives researched by Maslow. Comprehension is the second step up the ladder. Application is the third level and of critical importance because without application of knowledge, Going the Extra Mile only remains a mental concept and does not translate into the physical world. You must know about the concept first, understand what the concept means and why it is significant, and then actively apply the concept openly in your life in order to acquire the benefits.

You must take action in a variety of ways in order to achieve the desired results you want. The action taken must not be with the expectation of compensation from the recipient either. Your expectation of compensation comes from the Universe in perhaps ways unknown for now. The Universe is placed in your debt by Going the Extra Mile because you are engaging the natural laws of the Universe. Do good to do good and let it be. Your outcome or reward will be given from a different source. Trust me.

In this book, I will show you some of the means and methods of bringing this practice of Going the Extra Mile to immediate use in your own life. Each of us is distinct. We have different goals and objectives, but we have one thing in common. We live in the same world, and the world operates under unifying principles. The better we understand and accept these principles the better our outcome will be in life. We do not have to like it or understand it completely to benefit from it, but we have to accept it because it is the way the world works in which we live. When we want to better our own world, we must first understand the rules of the game we are playing in this game of life.

Story Time

Question: How do I personally apply this principle in my life and has it made a difference?

Answer: Absolutely. Professionally, I consider myself a person who works best in connecting others. I enjoy finding a need and filling it creatively and imaginatively. Some people would label me a hoarder, but I enjoy keeping things until I find the exact perfect need or use for them and am able to fill that need from my "collections."

I also am a "bookaholic" and my husband commented more than once that I have the Library of Congress on the bedroom floor. I enjoy reading as recreation and also for acquiring knowledge. My worldview widens as I read. My access to cultural appreciation and understanding expands as I read. And, my desire to do similar things in my lifetime such as caring for my pets, gardening, cooking, and trying out new things are all enhanced by reading. Reading is not passive. It is active. It engages the mind and promotes action.

I remember Don Green, the CEO/Executive Director for the Napoleon Hill Foundation, stating that when visiting homes without books he always understood why there was little personal initiative, little progress in taking the next steps to a better life-style. I agree with his assessment because books open doors to taking the first step outside of yourself that leads to a better future. That next step is Going the Extra Mile for yourself first and then for others.

Consider the fact that I am unable to cook a roast, bake a birthday cake, plan a celebratory dinner, host a reception, or do a variety of other things until I understand the process by doing it first for myself. One way to acquire this knowledge is through reading.

Don is right. Homes without reading material are the poorest homes of all. Once the ability to do is acquired, the next and most important step in the process is to *Do It Now!*

If you have not read the children's book, *Stone Soup*, look it up on the internet or at the library. It gives a concrete example of how small, rather insignificant contributions from everyone in the town, can make a huge difference for a meal that is not only wholesome but leads to better and less fearful communications among the members in the community.

In order to hit one out of the ballpark, we must use the tools of the game. Ready? Bat and ball in hand? Let's begin by beginning.

Do It Now!

Begin right here, right now, by doing these activities.

1. Invest in a 5 x 7 pack of note cards. Use one note card each day and record your Going the Extra Mile (GEM) activities. Do not be concerned with how many GEM activities you complete, but rather that you are doing them. Begin small, take notice, and then grow your good deeds.

2. Invest in a journal. Track your progress in developing the GEM principle. Record your thoughts, actions, and questions regarding this foundational principle. Create an image in your mind's eye by imagining what you are going to do in the future with this principle. Visualize yourself doing it. Dream big! And then *Do It Now!*

3. Write down three goals that you have for yourself in utilizing this principle in your daily life. Dream big. After all it is your life that is on the drawing board. Time to create a masterpiece.

Dreams are today's answers to tomorrow's questions.
—EDGAR CAYCE

The Little Things
of Living

*It is a curious fact that most people will do something to help
humanity, even when they wouldn't do it just to help you.*
—Napoleon Hill

It's the little things that count. The daily habits that
are performed over and over again lead to our character development. Thoughts lead to actions and actions
lead to results. If we are looking for good results, the
best advice is to hold positive thoughts that are followed by actions that enrich our life. Seems simple
enough, but sometimes even the simplest things can
be ignored or appear to be of no consequence in the
big picture that becomes our reality.

Considering that little things add up and become
big things, developing the habit of Going the Extra
Mile takes on greater significance because once we
realize that tiny episodes of daily giving increase not
only our effectiveness but our happiness in propor-
tion to our giving, the GEM Principle begins to be

comprehended and applied. The spirit of giving with no strings attached supplies the doer with more happiness and even fresh inspiration for doing more.

Opportunities to go the extra mile are individual enterprises. The practices that you perform cannot and do not have to be identical to those performed by others, but you can be inspired by them. Start small with the simple things. Look for opportunities to make a difference for someone else that is cost free, but significant.

Begin with words. Words that are sincere are cost free, but priceless. Notice something that has been done effectively and comment on how it affects you, appeals to you, and causes you to have a fresh perspective on things. Words that come from the heart can leave a lasting impression. They are the only gift that stays with us our entire lives.

Remember a compliment that you received. Maybe a teacher wrote on your paper "Best in the class," or told you that your art project will be put on display, or asked you to tutor another student because you grasped the lesson. By taking time to tell you that you merited praise, the words stayed with you for life. Your confidence soared, you were motivated to do even better, and the light of happiness burned inside you because another person noticed the good that was done. Likewise, when you praise another, you give this gift. The gift is a mutual one because you too feel the happiness given when you make the gesture.

I do not have to tell you that today's world is an anxious place. Instead of compliments we expect condemnations—someone telling us what we do wrong. This reverses any potential happiness and causes us to mutter similar thoughts regarding others. "Who do they think they are in criticizing me?" is usually a question we ask ourselves. When our attention shifts from praise to criticism our world is turned upside down in an instant and fault finding becomes the booty we seek. Strange isn't it? That certain words can lead us to acclaim or to destruction. It is essential that this process is understood because in Going the Extra Mile it is wrong to undercut, criticize, placate, scold, or terrorize another person and then expect positive results.

I am a reader and I enjoy reading works by all authors that shine a light in a positive direction. While working for the Napoleon Hill Foundation I have had the privilege of knowing people like Charlie Tremendous Jones and reading the works of others such as W. Clement Stone, Norman Vincent Peale, Dale Carnegie, Florence Scovel Shinn, Ella Wheeler Wilcox, Andrew Carnegie, Claude Bristol, Ralph Waldo Emerson, Henry David Thoreau, and more. Each of these writers influenced my thinking by their words, actions, and positive affirmations. I am aware that many people align these writers with the Prosperity Movement, and sometimes find fault with the approaches that are taken, but in my mind if each contributes an ounce of positivity to a person's life, it is the tiny light originating within their words that dispels the darkness. Why should we remain in the dark if even a spark of light can be provided? And the way forward can become illuminated.

Many of these writers parallel one or more of the researched principles of Dr. Napoleon Hill. His life's work was to determine what principles were consistently used in people's lives that contributed to their success. The 17 Principles are as follows:

1. Definiteness of Purpose
2. Master Mind Alliance
3. Applied Faith
4. Going the Extra Mile
5. Pleasing Personality
6. Personal Initiative
7. Positive Mental Attitude
8. Enthusiasm
9. Self-Discipline
10. Accurate Thinking
11. Controlled Attention
12. Teamwork
13. Learning from Adversity and Defeat
14. Creative Vision
15. Maintenance of Sound Health
16. Budgeting Time and Money
17. Cosmic Habitforce

That's it. All that is necessary to achieve whatever desire you have in life. Comprehensive. Complete. Concise. Dr. Hill's research contains historical references to numerous people who achieved success of their own choice and making in their chosen field. That is the composition of Dr. Hill's *Science of Success Course.* Nothing is more natural and consistent.

For example, Dale Carnegie emphasized *Pleasing Personality,* Claude Bristol wrote on *Applied Faith,* Norman Vincent Peale focused on *Positive Mental Attitude,* and Florence Scovel Shinn explored *Cosmic Habitforce.* Each of these writers and personalities knew that it was more constructive to focus on positive end results than it was to curse the darkness. Each always went the extra mile in informing their listeners and readers about their thoughts and feelings. In other words, they did not keep their candle hidden under a bushel basket—they wanted others to see the light.

Two individuals, Ella Wheeler Wilcox and Florence Scovel Shinn used their writing to influence people to condition their own minds for improved performance. Wilcox used poetry and Shinn used affirmations in helping students move toward more positive thinking. For example, in Wilcox's poem "The Winds of Fate" she writes:

> *One ship drives east and another drives west*
> *With the selfsame winds that blow.*
> *'Tis the set of the sails,*
> *And not the gales,*
> *That tell us the way to go.*

Like the winds of the sea are the ways of fate;
As we voyage along through life,
   'Tis the set of a soul
   That decides its goal,
And not the calm or the strife.

Wilcox's thoughts indicate that she believes that we can control our fate by how we set our sails—be it in a positive or negative manner.

Florence Scovel Shinn writes:

"Gratitude is the law of increase, and complaint is the law of decrease."

"The game of life is a game of boomerangs. Our thoughts, deeds and words return to us sooner or later with astounding accuracy."

"I do not limit God by seeing limitation in myself. With God and myself all things are possible."

"Do not neglect the day of small things, for little beginnings have big endings."

When considered, these thoughts can fill our mind and heart with the *Do It Now!* attitude because we can envision the positive end result. Florence Scovel Shinn so accurately states: "Your word is your wand. The words you speak create your own destiny." Amen to that thought.

Ralph Waldo Emerson writes: "Rings and jewels are not gifts, but apologies for gifts. The only gift is a portion of thyself." Based on Emerson's thought, consider how you can give a gift of spirit rather than substance. Here are some action starters:

1. Can you make a five minute phone call to someone who has not heard the phone ring in a week?
2. Can you congratulate someone on an achievement that may have gone unnoticed?
3. Can you recall and be thankful for the things that others have done for you?
4. Can you buy an extra item or two and donate it to a food bank?
5. Can you remember someone's birthday with kindness?
6. Can you pick up litter that you notice?
7. Can you support a cause you care about?
8. Can you write a positive message to another person?
9. Can you be kind to yourself?
10. Can you listen to another without interrupting their story?
11. Can you share a happy memory?
12. Can you make a person smile?
13. Can you feed someone the soul food of kindness?
14. Can you give something away that someone needs more than you do?
15. Can you thank people for the things they do for you?
16. Can you tell a joke?
17. Can you feed the birds and squirrels?

18. Can you assist another with pet clean up?
19. Can you anticipate a person's individual need and fill it?
20. Can you do the things only you can do to show encouragement, kindness, and understanding by boosting someone's ego?
21. Can you make a person's day by just being there and asking "what's new with you?"

Now, write your own "Can you do. . . ?" list that only you can do for another and then challenge yourself to complete the tasks. Perhaps you have been asked to extend some help in an area where only you are capable of helping. Begin here.

I remember a final call from Charlie Tremendous Jones and his focus on a book that I had written. The book is a compendium of poems by authors from around the time that Napoleon Hill wrote his classic book *Think and Grow Rich*. The book is entitled *Poems that Inspire You to Think and Grow Rich*. I wrote the book because of numerous inquiries that I received regarding quoted lines in *Think and Grow Rich* by Napoleon Hill. Readers wanted to know the source of many of the quotes or references contained in Hill's works.

Charlie Jones talked to me about the book and stated that he wished that he had read it sooner. What a kind comment from a gentleman who surely had other things more pressing on his mind than my book. That was the last call I had from him, and I always will treasure his remarks. His trademark quote encapsulates it all: "You will be the same person in five years as you are today except for the people you meet and the books you read." I am truly glad that I was fortunate enough to meet Charlie T. Jones and to read his books. His positive mental attitude changed my outlook on life. In his lectures he made people smile and laugh. His hugs and enthusiastic greetings were worth the wait. His message endures yet today.

Another mentor/employer I have is Don Green. Don operates in a different capacity. He is always forward looking, time sensitive, and can be demanding. But, from a person who often waits or delays a project, Don's intercession can be beneficial because he becomes the little voice inside my head that says "Do it Now." His motivation always is getting the job done, and I strongly appreciate his encouragement and insight. As soon as one project is finished, he is on to the next one. He is definitely a person who lives in the present with an eye to the future! Don has taught me many things, but one of the biggest lessons is not to procrastinate. *Do It Now!* is time sensitive and has real meaning for Don. I always feel that Don is looking over my shoulder reminding me to *Do It Now!* so that I can get on to the next thing. Progress not perfection is a slogan that I believe he incorporates into his daily living.

Claude Bristol is an author who wrote *The Magic of Believing.* I enjoy the book because it talks about Applied Faith. Many individuals lack applied faith not because they are disbelievers, but because they do not put their belief into action. Action is always the key. Without action we are told faith is dead. Also, without action our progress is dead as well. Bristol's work is spiritually based and that may not be of liking or interest to some people. For me, I find his ideas and research to be helpful and an inspiration to action. Bristol states:

> Your thoughts, those that predominate, determine your character, your career, indeed your everyday life. Thus it becomes easy to understand what is meant by the statement that a man's thoughts make or break him. And when we realize that there can be no action or reaction, either good or bad, without the generating force of thought initiating it, the Biblical saying, "For whatsoever a man soweth, that shall he also reap," and Shakespeare's words, "There is nothing either good or bad, but thinking makes it so," become more intelligible.

As you can tell, I could go on and on about people who contribute to my inspiration, and I encourage you to keep a list of past and current people who inspire you. When Napoleon Hill teaches the principle of a Mastermind Alliance he reminds us that those individuals in our "alliance" can be from the past or present. The only requirement is that they have something to offer the group in the form of advice.

My Mastermind Alliance consists of writers, family, and teachers who may have physically moved on but are still alive in my memory and thoughts and therefore can offer me advice as if they were physically alive. I think that you can admit too that if someone close to you has died, you still speak to them. I do, and I also ask for their help and direction. These ancestors still have our best interests at heart. If their advice was credible while they lived on the Earth plane, it will be just as credible now from their current viewpoint.

So far I have mentioned several other principles that Dr. Hill includes in his *Science of Success Course.* Why? Because these principles all work in tandem just as our body does. We are composed of systems that independently could not operate separately from the others. These include our digestive system, our endocrine system, our circulatory system, our skeletal system, our respiratory system, our immune system, our excretory system, our urinary system, our muscular system, our digestive system, our nervous system and our reproductive system. In order to exist, they must function as a unit. So too does the Science of Success. Without each integral part, the process lacks coherence and complexity.

As you will begin to discover, Going the Extra Mile is only one of the 17 Success Principles, but importantly one of the Big Four that tops Hill's list. The Big Four are essential principles since without each of them working in unison we can become disabled in our journey toward success. A chair lacking a leg cannot balance or be of service on its own.

Likewise without the four cornerstones of success, a critical support piece would be missing.

Let's review once more why beginning at the beginning and keeping it simple is a good place to start in learning about what contributes to a person's successful outcomes. Assuming that happiness, contentment, tolerance, appreciation, understanding, kindness and finances are all outcomes a person may seek from the journey in life, it is beneficial to now ask yourself the definition of success that is meaningful and fulfilling to you and why.

Begin to jot some ideas down noticing what is gratifying to you and makes you happy and gives you a feeling of fulfillment in life. This definition will be different for each of us because we are unique and have different gifts to offer to others and the world. Therefore, our focus will be different and not a cookie cutter approach to success. If, for example, care for the environment resonates with you, then look at what contributions you might make to improved environmental concerns. Or, if animal rights appeal to you and you have a strong desire to make a difference in this area, what actions can you take now to show your support?

The time is here to start the process of discerning what is of major importance to you and what is of a lesser concern. Focus on those things that you have a passion for and that draw you in to make a positive difference. These objectives will help you later on as you create a plan for delving deeper into Going the Extra Mile.

Recently I did a display entitled "Turn Darkness into Light." I was aware of this theme from Ireland's *Book of Kells* that is displayed at Trinity College in Dublin. At the time the Monks illustrated the book based upon the gospels from Biblical text, the written word was "dark," and any light brought to the mechanism of copying the words had to be an act of creative imagination on the part of the individual Monk copying the text. But, with colorful illustrations, the *Book of Kells* began an artistic approach to the beauty of the written work.

Adding color is one way to bring darkness to light, but there are others. Working within their milieu and with what they had at hand, these Monks who were in many cases teenagers, found beauty and passion in what they had to work with in terms of materials. And, for that the world is forever grateful.

Likewise, in our own areas we can turn darkness into light through creativity and imagination. What is it that each of us can do alone or together in order to make this world a better place in which to live? That is ultimately the question that we are placed on this planet to answer. Each answer is the unique expression of ourselves and what we individually have to offer. That is the key to uncovering our definite major purpose in this life.

Below are a few testimonies from individuals who tell us how and why they take the simple approach of Going the Extra Mile. When you read what they have written, perhaps you can begin to uncover their definite major purpose in life.

> *The greatest of all gifts is the gift of an*
> *opportunity for one to help himself.*
> —NAPOLEON HILL

In my accounting practice, Going the Extra Mile was sometimes something as simple as personally calling a client on the phone to remind them that filing deadlines were approaching, or driving to their homes to deliver tax returns when it would have been very inconvenient for them to come to my office. Other times, Going the Extra Mile meant staying up at night working on a report the client had to have the next morning, even though I only received the source documents the night before!

People need to feel they are important. Going the extra mile for your clients or your boss is the best way to let them know they are important to you and that you'll make extra efforts on their behalf.

As Dr. Hill pointed out, most people aren't willing to go the first mile, let alone the extra mile. Incorporating the philosophy of Going the Extra Mile into your work ethic is one of the best ways to ensure that you will come out on top in even the most competitive business or work environments.   —Eliezer A. Alperstein

*The one and only thing any man has to give in return
for the material riches he desires is useful service.*
—NAPOLEON HILL

A wise person once said that "to know a man you must first walk a mile in his shoes." How powerful a statement it is to say to another that you are prepared to go an extra mile for them in your own shoes! You do this for them—not for you.

I have been teaching in an all-boys disadvantaged city school in the Republic of Ireland for several years. Dr. Hill's philosophy has been a huge part of my students' lives for the past two years. This is all due to the application of the principle of Going the Extra Mile. My first true encounter of this principle at work was during my initial contact with Judy Williamson at the Napoleon Hill World Learning Center. Having explained my circumstances to her and having relayed the stories of my students constantly struggling to find a compass for life, Judy stepped up to the mark and said, "Phillip, I will walk this journey with you and together we will show your students the way."

That way is Dr. Hill's way—a path of purpose, determination, and success. I have now completed two years of teaching Napoleon Hill's philosophy to my students and already the transformation in some of their lives is truly astounding! My students all know that through living out the principle of Going the Extra Mile, they have a new set of tools for life—a compass to guide them and a principle to live by. "Do unto others as you would have them do unto you." If you can't go the extra mile with someone, then go it for them! You always get that mile back in spades. Judy's tiny light of hope has lit the fires of purpose and success in souls who otherwise may have been consigned to walk the path of life alone.　　　—Philip McCauley

> *Happiness may be had only*
> *by helping others to find it.*
> —NAPOLEON HILL

I learned from my grandmother how to always make the most of my time and to apply myself during the whole day. When visiting her on the farm, I saw how she was always productive—not busy, but producing much with her time. Farmers are a wonderful example of individuals who apply themselves at the crack of dawn, when the rooster crows, and retiring when the sun sets. One of the reasons is because they have to work with nature, where standards and principles are set in divine order. The other reason is simply because of the love and joy of what nature has to offer each day. Mother Nature always goes the extra mile, producing more than is needed, and I believe we should follow that example in our lives.

—Loretta Levin

> *First of all, Going the Extra Mile calls*
> *the law of increasing returns into action.*
> —NAPOLEON HILL

Going the Extra Mile will also pave the way for you to get the promotion and monetary rewards you are aiming for. "Extra mile" here means the investment you make in yourself by acquiring new skills and knowledge that are relevant to your job. You should perform this "software upgrade" voluntarily, even if your company does not provide such training. Your additional skill set will differentiate you from your colleagues and you will be the natural choice for promotion when the opportunity arises.

Remember this, opportunities only come to those who are prepared and ready to receive them. To be successful, you must have that something extra that makes you different. By reading this passage now, you are already Going the Extra Mile. If you continue this path, your life will never be the same.   —Tan Juan Keat

> *Adopt the habit as a part of your life's philosophy,*
> *and let it become known by all who know you that*
> *you render such service out of choice, not as a matter*
> *of accident, but by deliberate intent, and soon you*
> *will see keen competition for your service.*
> —NAPOLEON HILL

All my life I have done whatever it took to help people in any way that my God-given talents would allow me to do. Whether it was helping students be as successful in my classroom as they possibly could, or helping my children develop into honest, loving, and independent individuals, my life has been devoted to being a caring and sharing spouse and lending a helping hand to my friends or whomever I could. Going the extra mile helped me achieve the best I could be.

—Rose Wright

As can be read in the above testimonials, we do not have to reinvent the wheel each time we want to duplicate a success. The Going the Extra Mile principle allows us to shine when we intentionally donate our time and talents to someone else.

Sometimes just acknowledging that you have a little gift for someone brightens both of your days. In this way Going the Extra Mile becomes a reciprocal process that fosters good rapport. Keep in mind that in order to get better results you always want to render more service and better service. That is the extra spoonful of goodness that makes the end result all that much sweeter for both the recipient and yourself.

As we are learning, the little things of everyday living do make a big difference in our lives over-all. Practicing what we know to bring good results insures our future. The Law of Increasing Returns comes into play the moment we begin taking action and also activates the Law of Compensation in our favor when we go the extra mile in a positive frame of mind with no expectation of compensation. The formula is simple and it is the only equation in the *Science of Success Course.*

$$Q1 + Q2 + MA = C$$

Quality of Service rendered

+

Quantity of Service rendered

+

Mental Attitude in which it is rendered

=

Your **Compensation** in the world and
the amount of space you will occupy
in the hearts of your fellowmen.

A note from Dr. Hill:

The word *compensation* in this formula means all the things that come into your life: money, joy, happiness, harmony in human relations, spiritual enlightenment, peace of mind, a positive mental attitude, the capacity for faith, the ability and desire to share blessings with others, a mind that is open and receptive to truth on all subjects, a sense of tolerance and fair play, and any other praiseworthy attitude or attribute you may seek.

Ponder the above explanation of compensation and consider how your actions bring one or more of these things about in your life. Remember that balance is the key to successful living. If you only focus on financial rewards you will be neglecting the true riches of life that entitle you to every happiness worth achieving.

Story Time

Question: Do the little things of life really add up to make a critical difference in our outcomes in life?

Answer: I believe so. When we put our best foot forward, doors are opened that otherwise would have remained closed. When we connect with people, the same people bring opportunities that would have never found a path to our door. A few years ago I was made aware of an opportunity to travel to Uganda with a church group by a man who was doing repairs at my home. In casual conversation I talked about my love of traveling, and he remembered this. He mentioned an upcoming trip and thought that I might be interested in checking it out. I followed up on his suggestion, made the trip, and have new memories and experiences of the people I met and learned from in Uganda. Consequently, I hope to return someday and learn more about the country and continent.

Once when traveling to Ireland, Don Green decided to accompany our group at the last minute. He enjoyed the getaway experience especially the Irish countryside, rainbows, nutritious food, and the "tidy towns." Tidy Towns are those towns that receive recognition for being the tidiest and cleanest in the area—minus litter. Don said that we could learn a great deal from our Irish neighbors in this regard. And, he indicates to me that he would like to return one day.

When we take the time to go the extra mile for ourselves we always bring back home much more than we contributed. I like to accompany people who have never traveled to a foreign country and watch their awareness grow as they experience new things through new eyes. Literally, by Going the Extra Mile, we grow and expand our awareness. By doing what we have always done, we get what we have always got. No big deal. But, by venturing out to places unknown we always receive more. Whether it's by going to a new restaurant, a new city, a new state, or even a new country, our vision is expanded. Risky, yes. But beneficial, always.

Do It Now!

Begin right here, right now, by doing these activities.
1. What GEM actions are you prepared to take today?
2. Visualize yourself completing them.
3. Once completed, note the responses from the recipients, if any, on your daily note card.
4. Tonight reread your list and consider whether or not you might take the same or similar actions again tomorrow but with different people.

5. Reread this chapter highlighting words, phrases, or sentences that are significant to you.

6. Write an affirmation. For example: *Today I am determined to make a difference in the lives of myself and others by Going the Extra Mile.* Repeat it throughout the day to yourself.

7. Before falling asleep, think of the things that happened today. Express your appreciation to the Universe for all the good you gave to others and all the good others gave to you. Do this nightly.

If you want to lift yourself up,
lift someone else up.
—Booker T. Washington

Chapter 3

The Service Essentials

The place to begin is in your own mind.
Your success and failure are in your own mind.
—Napoleon Hill

The basic principles of success are ripe with potential possibilities but only if you lay the correct groundwork with the right mental attitude. Good and Evil are two opposing forces in the world and each force can be cultivated for the right or for the wrong reasons. In order to operationalize the outcomes you want, you must engage in the work that produces the correct series of outcomes. By Going the Extra Mile with sincerity of forethought and expectation of positive results you engage the workings of the Universe in your behalf by putting it on notice.

You expect that your actions will produce good results for yourself and others. Consequently, these results become outcomes that position you for the compensation you deserve and are entitled to expect. Through your clear thinking combined with immediate actions you are sending a powerful message to the Universe that you are laying the groundwork for your current and future rewards.

In *The Magic of Believing*, Claude Bristol writes:

> I am cognizant of the fact that there are powerful forces at work in this country that would dominate us, substituting a kind of regimentation for the competitive system which has made America great among nations. They would attempt to destroy individual thinking and initiative, cherished ever since our Pilgrim Fathers established this country in defiance of Old World tyranny. I believe that we must continue to retain the wealth of spirit of our forefathers, for if we don't we shall find ourselves dominated in everything we do by a mighty few and shall become serfs in fact if not in name.

This book was copyrighted in 1948, two years before I was born, but the above paragraph could have been written today. The message is clear. Individual thinking and doing must be tantamount to a life worth living.

Dr. Hill recognized and subsequently researched and revealed his findings on what constitutes success. Without critical thinking and thoughtful application the freedom people desire is at risk. Dr. Hill has determined the pathway, but only you can determine your outcome. Every single step creates opportunity for advancement. Consider the parts of the Success Equation below.

The $Q1 + Q2 + MA = C$ formula is based upon the letters beginning with each step.

The **Quality** of Service rendered means that what you have to offer is worthy of someone's receipt. If you give away throwaways or castoffs that have no value to yourself or others, the quality of your service is negligible. In others words, no one is interested in something you do not want yourself. Rather, your gifts of service need to be given freely from the heart and worthy of being received.

The **Quantity** of Service rendered means that what you offer is not too little or too late. Help that is overdue, too late, or not enough has little significance in substance. It is the quantity of service rendered at the proper time that hits the mark. *Do It Now!* is the proper message here before it arrives too late and is meaningless.

The **Mental Attitude** in which the service is rendered causes the gift to either be lackluster or star studded. Something begrudgingly given or given in a selfish manner negates the equation. It is not the amount, but the spirit that determines the appropriateness and value of the gift.

The **Compensation** is what weight your gift holds in the Universe. The widow's mite was all she could afford, yet her gift was among the best because she gave what she had in the right mental attitude. We are not to judge the merit of someone's gift. That is left to a higher power. Padre Pio, an Italian Saint, used the smallest gift he received as the cornerstone coin in the building of his free hospital in his hometown. Nothing is too small to have tremendous purpose and merit.

As you think through this equation you may begin to better understand and appreciate that more is at play here than simply Going the Extra Mile. Someone who understands this principle engages the mind, heart, and spirit of the philosophy by participating in an action that improves the world for another. This is a concept that the Science of Success underscores as a predominate tenet of use.

This means that the Science of Success not only works in your behalf but in the behalf of others that you engage and service in the process. A new beginning is a head start for each of you. Nothing works unless you do, and when you do you put into motion the beneficial powers of the Universe.

Napoleon Hill states that "thoughts are things." Ponder this concept because your thoughts are energy and what you put out in the form of thought vibrations are what you attract to you because like attracts like. This is an extremely important concept because giving—as in Going the Extra Mile—sets off an action of receiving.

Whatever you are thinking or feeling attracts to you like metal to a magnet that which is present in your mind. Now, add the physical dimension of taking action and operationalizing these thoughts or feelings and you engage the fundamental law of the

Universe—Newton's Law. For every action there is a reaction.

In seeking good outcomes it is only common sense to believe that these good actions will rebound to you in much the same manner as when a farmer is paid well over his investment in the seeds that he plants. This occurs through the crop that he harvests. If the harvest is a successful one, the farmer will be rewarded an outcome that is many times over his initial investment.

The repetition of Going the Extra Mile in your daily living causes these actions to advance to a new you created by these daily habits of giving. This "habitizing" force becomes second nature soon and requires less conscious thought. The practices advance to the level of the subconscious mind and your constant giving engages the process of receiving on your behalf. As we give fully and freely we enrich ourselves and set off the process that becomes a conduit for both giving and receiving.

It does not matter what good you do—be it small or large—what matters most is that you do it in order to discover the "to do" that matters most. You adopt this process and follow through on your own initiative needing no one's permission to do so. When you develop the practice and catch the spirit of the ideas you will witness big changes as you detect the secret that this principle holds.

In the meantime, follow the directions and continue to go the extra mile for no other purpose than to spread your giving in the right mental attitude with quality and quantity of service. Equalize your giving and burn no bridges if a recipient does not respond to your gift. It may take time for the giving of yourself to others in whatever form makes sense in the moment, but by doing so you will uncover hidden benefits that would have remained hidden had you not taken the action your intuition told you to take.

In deciding what to do in Going the Extra Mile, do not deliberate too long. Take the leap and do what seems needed to be done for those you identify as needing it the most. Simple things lead to big outcomes and no gentle favor ever goes unrewarded in the Universe. "What goes around comes around," and "do the thing and you will have the power," are two sayings that bear repeating because they are truisms. Thoughts lead to actions and actions lead to outcomes, either good or bad. By regulating and conditioning your thoughts you are creating new habits that will bring good results when they are manifested in the physical world. Think on these things, and you will begin to understand why cultivating a second nature of giving as a habit will prepare you to understand the three other cornerstone principles of Definiteness of Purpose, Mastermind Alliance, and Applied Faith.

As a further means of clarification, it might be an appropriate time to consider the power of your conscious and subconscious minds and how all this comes into direct correlation with Going the Extra Mile. As you begin to work practically and constructively with this principle you are helping sensitize your mind to accepting what it is you want in life. By focusing on the positive, you are channeling a positive message to your waking mind and also to your subconscious mind.

Both minds are important, but they undertake different duties or jobs in different degrees. We all know about our conscious mind. It operates off the information that we receive from our five senses: seeing, hearing, tasting, smelling, and touching. The major powers of our conscious mind are reason, logic, judgment, and a moral sense of right and wrong. This mind is called our waking mind because it operates while we are awake and is the source of our waking thoughts.

The subconscious mind has far greater powers. It never sleeps. It is on the job 24/7 and works to maintain all our bodily functions as well as most importantly intuition, imagination, and suggestion. Some people believe that it aligns with Universal Intelligence in the past, present, and future. You can call upon the powers of your subconscious mind by having absolute faith and belief in what you are asking to receive and know that you are capable of handling it. The subconscious mind works in the present through visualization and imagery. Imprint images on your mind's eye with a positive mental expectation that they have already happened, and before you know it, these images will become reality.

In order to utilize this powerhouse of wisdom you must envision what it is you desire as already accomplished. Otherwise, your belief of something happening sometime in the future someday will be just that. Something, sometime, someday. Not today. Therefore, when engaging your subconscious mind to work in your behalf you must envision the picture perfect end result that you have attained. The perfect job, the perfect companion, the perfect home, perfect health, etc. By doing this you draw, through what may seem like coincidences to others, those things that will enable these results to happen in the here and now.

For example, have you ever had a strong desire for something that you want, but have not attained? You may have thought on this topic for a long time, seeing yourself finding, buying and using the item in question. You enhance your desire for this object by allowing your thinking (conscious mind) to dwell on this seeming daydream. However, you are certain that it will show up sooner or later in your life. And it always does, but not in the way you may have imagined, but show up it does. Using your intuition you have conditioned your subconscious mind to independently seek out this desire. When the outcome is revealed to you as to how you may acquire this item, you need to act on it at once. If you wait, think it is just a pipe dream, you will be correct.

Doubting your subconscious mind causes nothing to happen. Following its directive can have the potential to change your life. By listening to that still, small voice inside that says "turn this way, not that," you begin to trust your intuition and believe in the best outcome for yourself.

Historically individuals such as Shakespeare, Dickens, St. Teresa of Avila, Florence Nightingale, Emerson, Tesla, Einstein, Edison, Freud, Jung, Jesus, and others who excelled beyond ordinary living have tapped into the power of the subconscious mind. So critical is it that without this skill and realization of the powerhouse that is inside each of us, you may never reach your full potential. Napoleon Hill details the difference between our two minds below with this example:

> The subconscious mind may be likened to an automobile, while the conscious mind may be considered the driver. The power is in the automobile—not the driver. The driver learns to release and control the power in the motor. In the same way, a person may learn how to tap the power of the subconscious mind and direct it into channels of his own choosing. The conscious mind is the architect; the subconscious mind is the vast storehouse from which may be requisitioned the mental materials for the project which is under construction. The conscious mind makes the plan and decides what shall be done. The subconscious mind develops the power to do it.

By introducing these concepts early on in the study of Going the Extra Mile, you will become aware that you are conditioning your mind for expanded awareness. It takes continued practice to engage the subconscious mind, and you are at the doorway to experiencing flashes of intuition that will direct you most consistently toward your goal. Once given the insight it is of great importance that you take action by expressing gratitude for this gift of direction.

Napoleon Hill has written a creed for riches that he suggests is to be recited daily, or more often, as a prayer of thankfulness for that which you have received or are receiving. You might commit it to memory or write it on a note card and place it where it is readily available for reading at various times throughout the day. Its purpose is to prepare our conscious mind and notify our subconscious mind that we are ready to receive in abundance what the Universe has to offer. Napoleon Hill's words appear below.

> I give thanks daily, not for mere riches, but for wisdom with which to recognize, embrace, and properly use the great abundance of riches I now have at my command. I have no enemies because I injure no man for any cause, but I try to benefit all with whom I come in contact, by teaching them the way to enduring riches. I have more material wealth than I need because I am free from greed and covet only the material things I can use while I live.

In 1916, Rev. William J. H. Boetcker authored a list of Ten "Cannots." By reading through them, you might gain some insight as to another approach that can be taken in your quest to go the extra mile in today's age. It appears that each "cannot" today could be the substance of a much needed debate.

1. You cannot bring about prosperity by discouraging thrift.
2. You cannot strengthen the weak by weakening the strong.
3. You cannot help the poor man by destroying the rich.
4. You cannot further brotherhood of man by inciting class hatred.
5. You cannot build character and courage by taking away a man's initiative.
6. You cannot help small men by tearing down big men.
7. You cannot lift the wage earner by pulling down the wage payer.
8. You cannot keep out of trouble by spending more than your income.
9. You cannot establish security on borrowed money.
10. You cannot help men permanently by doing for them what they will not do for themselves.

Consider that this list brings into focus Napoleon Hill's admonition "to injure no man for any cause, but try to benefit all with whom I come in contact, by teaching them the way to enduring riches."

As you are beginning to understand, each and every individual is the person responsible for their own success or failure in this lifetime. There is a science to success and you can program yourself for this course by beginning to perform the activities that will put the Universe in your debt. Going the Extra Mile is one of the beginning step that opens doors to understanding how this entire success philosophy works in your behalf. As you begin at the beginning, make certain that you have a strong desire, better yet an emotionalized burning desire for this type of life goal that will bring you the outcome you desire. A cold, half-baked, here today gone tomorrow desire never places anyone on the success beam.

Napoleon Hill states that "thought plus action equals success." But, if you want to achieve success in a quicker fashion you might consider adding one little word—"emotionalized." Making the formula read: Thought plus EMOTIONALIZED action equals success. Why emotionalized action? Because that single powerful word is the language that speaks to your subconscious mind. When you feel it in your emotions, when it becomes an obsession, when you eat, sleep, and dream it in your daily living, you will bring it about because you have put your subconscious mind on notice that you already have this and as sure as night follows the day it will happen.

Dr. Hill details the ten basic motives that propel all people worldwide to action. Consider which one inspires you to an emotionalized pitch of readiness. That one motive may be just the kingpin in the success formula that pushes you to take action. Consider the motives below and next pick the one that is your number one motive for taking action.

1. The desire for self-preservation.
2. The emotion of love.
3. The emotion of fear.
4. The emotion of sex.
5. The desire for life after death.
6. The desire for freedom of body and mind.
7. The desire for revenge.
8. The emotion of hate.
9. The desire for self-expression and recognition.
10. The desire for material gain.

Please remember to be cautious with the desire for revenge and the emotion of hate. The philosophy will work for good or evil, but by maintaining only positive intents will the good in life be returned to you and magnified. Evil has its own "rewards."

Giving begets living and living is done through sharing. As we go the extra mile in sharing our resources, we condition ourselves for the reception of something more. By hoarding, being selfish, failing to reach out to others, not doing what we are capable of doing, the goodness that would come to us is blocked. I am not saying that it is easy to be a person who continually gives themselves away for causes, duties, jobs, etc., but if you refuse to be of service you are creating a bottleneck or stopper that prevents the flow of goodness from coming to you.

Biblically we are told to "do unto others as you would have others do unto you." It seems simple enough to abide by this rule, but the proof is in the doing. Reflect on the following poem often attributed to Mother Teresa, but actually written by Kent M. Keith.

The Paradoxical Commandments

People are unreasonable, illogical, and self-centered.
Love them anyway.
If you do good, people may accuse you of selfish motives.
Do good anyway.
If you are successful, you may win
false friends and true enemies.
Succeed anyway.
The good you do today may be forgotten tomorrow.
Do good anyway.
Honesty and transparency make you vulnerable.
Be honest and transparent anyway.
What you spend years building
may be destroyed overnight.
Build anyway.
People who really want help
may attack you if you help them.
Help them anyway.
Give the world the best you have and you may get hurt.
Give the world your best anyway.

Emily Dickinson writes:

> *If I can stop one heart from breaking,*
> *I shall not live in vain;*
> *If I can ease one life the aching,*
> *Or cool one pain,*
> *Or help one fainting robin*
> *Unto his nest again,*
> *I shall not live in vain.*

Begin at the beginning and take charge of doing one or more of the things that the writers recommend and I guarantee that your life will be the richer for it.

The saying, "it's the little things that count" is a truism in this success philosophy. Little things—actions—accumulate and become big things as they are performed in the right mental attitude.

In the last chapter, we began by laying the *groundwork for success.* Let's continue again with more constructive techniques.

Story time

Question: Does your subconscious mind speak to you?

Answer: Yes, my subconscious mind speaks to me and I attempt to hold it in conversation. By that I mean when I encounter a problem, a dead end, an impasse, or am just frustrated about something, I ask for assistance in solving the problem or concern right before going to sleep. I remind myself the subconscious mind connects with the Universal Mind and holds all potential answers to life's problems. Upon waking, any dreams, images, impressions, or directions in the form of lingering intuitions, coincidences, synchronicities, or leads I have I take seriously and put them to use.

All the problems out there have answers if we truly look for resolutions, and act to make them happen. It may not be a one step process, and it could take several steps, but if undertaken the outcome will meet our requirements.

Solutions are there for the taking, and if we pursue any given objective with emotionalized thinking, the answer will be revealed to us.

After my husband died, there were many things that I felt that I was unable to do regarding finances, home maintenance, everyday living, and moving forward with my life. From cutting the grass to filing taxes, I was a neophyte in the process. When asking my subconscious mind for a remedy, I always followed its guidance and achieved positive outcomes. When friends and family said it couldn't be done, I did not accept that fate. Today, almost six years later, I know where to turn if help is needed. For the most part I can do it now for myself due to the guidance that I have received from others coupled with following the directives from my subconscious mind.

Do It Now!

Begin right here, right now, by doing these activities.

1. What have you been doing differently this week that you have not done before? What results do you notice? Same or different?

2. Continue the practice of writing out the daily note cards and actions taken for Going the Extra Mile.

3. Note the results beneath the actions taken.

4. What benefits are in it for you? Why do it?

5. Reread this chapter highlighting words, phrases, or sentences that are significant to you.

6. Consider your two minds. Visualize what you want in the here and now. See yourself achieving your goals one goal at a time.

7. Have you noticed any messages from your *subconscious mind* to your *conscious mind?* Have you acted on any of these?

8. Before falling asleep, think of the things that happened today. Express your appreciation to the Universe for all the good you gave to others and all the good others gave to you.

I believe that if one always looked at the skies,
one would end up with wings.
—GUSTAVE FLAUBERT

Chapter 4

The Spirit of Service

When you have talked yourself into
what you want, right there is the place to
stop talking and begin saying it with deeds.
—NAPOLEON HILL

A man's best recommendation is that which
he gives himself . . . by rendering superior
service in the right mental attitude.
—NAPOLEON HILL

By Going the Extra Mile daily you begin to receive Compensation from the Universe in ways expected and unexpected. Be on the alert to recognize that Dr. Hill's Twelve Riches of Life are showing up more frequently as you are now on the success beam and on the lookout for them.

The Twelve Riches of Life are:
1. A Positive Mental Attitude
2. Sound Physical Health
3. Harmony in Human Relationships
4. Freedom from Fear

5. The Hope of Achievement
6. The Capacity for Faith
7. Willingness to Share One's Blessings
8. A Labor of Love
9. An Open Mind on All Subjects
10. Self-Discipline
11. The Capacity to Understand People
12. Financial Security

When you are Going the Extra Mile by providing more and better service than you are paid to do, you are immediately compensated in some or all of these twelve areas. Let's discuss each of the Twelve Riches and their relationship to Going the Extra Mile. Going the Extra Mile daily tallies up to a multitude of riches.

1. A Positive Mental Attitude: By Going the Extra Mile you cancel the thought of negativity and decide to do whatever is necessary to bring about enrichment in your life and that of others. This very act shines back on you and your attitude benefits from the action as well. Rather than considering all the reasons something cannot be done, you take a step in a positive direction and thereby move in that direction yourself both consciously and subconsciously.

2. Sound Physical Health: Endorphins respond to action. By being active rather than passive you condition yourself for better daily health practices. Physically, our bodies appreciate the movement and the motivation. Helping others can create a healing attitude in your own life. You become more optimistic and thereby have better outcomes when dealing with your own health issues.

3. Harmony in Human Relationships: By reaching out to others we strive for and create mutual understanding. By focusing on the good in ourselves and those around us, more pleasure is received from life. And, this equates to less stress. Less stress is a critical factor in the Maintenance of Sound Health.

4. Freedom from Fear: The directive "Do the thing and you will have the power," works to banish fear and creates a sense of well-being. Try it and see for yourself. The world is not simply all either/or, good/bad, light/dark, but a balance that we can create by facing our fears and moving beyond them.

5. The Hope of Achievement: Having something to work for and look forward to aids in the productivity needed to achieve positive outcomes. When you work on something you love to do, you really never work a day in your life.

6. The Capacity for Faith: Being able to believe in something greater than yourself promotes a sense of security in today's world. People experience less depression and exhibit a more positive attitude when they have a faith based belief system.

7. Willingness to Share One's Blessings: It is in giving that we receive. The more we give, the more comes back to us.

8. A Labor of Love: Doing something productive with our time and talent that we enjoy doing and would do even if not paid.

9. An Open Mind on All Subjects: Being a lifelong learner. Never believing that education is finite.

10. Self-Discipline: Compelling yourself to do the work that needs to be done when necessary.

11. The Capacity to Understand People: Getting along with people in all walks of life for the purpose of the betterment of yourself and humanity.

12. Financial Security: Knowing that financial stability will come into your life as you engage the Twelve Riches and expecting nothing less.

Knowing and doing are two separate entities. We can know all of the above practices cognitively but unless they are put into action in a spirit of harmony, no results will follow. Often we can become confused about the Spirit of Service in Going the Extra Mile and find it difficult to hone in on a proper need and fill it. We may question ourselves about doing something and argue ourselves right out of the process because we may feel there is a conflict with our morals, values and beliefs. This can become a crutch for not doing, rather than a rationale for being of service. Let me explain.

Many belief systems espouse the corporal works of mercy that are practiced worldwide. Feeding the hungry, housing the homeless, providing clothing for those in need, spending time with the sick, visiting the imprisoned, giving to the poor, and caring for the terminally ill and dying are the seven areas that are generally mentioned.

Too often when a plea goes out for help in these areas, one response may be to donate money to a cause and believe that is enough. Although it is a start, it is insufficient because we never get our hands dirty. Now is a good time to consider how you might go beyond a cash donation and take the next step in immersing yourself in one or more of these areas of need. It does not have to be something as dramatic as joining the Peace Corps, but it does have to have incremental steps that lead to something more. Idea starters might be the following:

Feeding the Hungry

- Making sure your immediate and extended families are being properly nourished. Fast food diets, processed foods, poor eating habits, inability to prepare meals or no desire to cook healthy meals all contribute to improper nutrition. Be of service in these areas by making certain healthy dietary habits are promoted at home, at work, and in your community.

- Volunteer at food kitchens or places of food distribution that help needy families.
- Read about local and world hunger and educate yourself as to how you can make a difference by understanding the food chain process.
- Waste less food.

Housing the Homeless
- Help the needy and elderly maintain the homes they already have.
- Work within your community to provide low income housing.
- Provide support in building housing for those in need and participate in recovery processes for those undergoing natural disasters.

Clothing Those in Need
- Donate gently used clothing to agencies that assist those in need for no or low cost.
- Work an afternoon or two weekly for an agency that distributes clothing.
- Assist in separating, labeling, and boxing clothing shipped to areas of need.

Visiting the Sick
- Be conscientious about visiting the sick. If not in person, by phone.

- Provide relief for a caregiver by offering time to relieve them for a few hours.
- Deliver food and medications to the homebound. Drive those in need of transportation to appointments.

Visiting the Imprisoned

- Support training that enables prisoners to acquire skills for use on release.
- Support chaplains who minister to those in prison.
- Support programs for prisoners with families. At holiday times these interventions are crucial.

Providing for the Poor

- Contribute to those in need through registered charities.
- Sponsor programs to raise funds for local organizations that give to the poor.
- Round up at the cash register for groups that you recognize and know provide good services.

Assisting with the Terminally Ill

- Visit the ill and their families.
- Spend time with the survivors.
- Make phone calls to those who are grieving.
- Send cards of condolence to the families of those who have died. Include a positive recollection about the person for the family to read.

You may not be comfortable in addressing each of these areas, but the general idea is to find one need that you are passionate about and fill it. This will lead to another, and yet another need to be filled. Take it slow and easy, but do the activity, reflect upon it, and see how it develops in your life. Remember, fill the need as described, not as you see it or determine it needs to be done. The point is to get outside of yourself and reach out to others in a pre-determined, helpful manner.

For myself, I have done volunteer work in schools, communities, and prisons. I also donate funds when unable to participate fully myself, but I consider where my financial donation will make the most good. I taught prison classes for the Napoleon Hill Foundation and Purdue University Calumet at nearby prisons and always felt that I learned more than I taught.

Years ago I was asked by a mentor to teach a class at a local prison for a professor who had died. I did, and I believe that I am the better for it. I went on to teach several classes and never regretted my decision. Legally, you cannot maintain any outside contact with the prisoners during or after their release, but I never doubted that something in the semester long class assisted their transition when they returned to the outside world. This being said, had I not accepted the opportunity, I never would have had the experience and I never would have grown as well in the process. Take the challenge, it is a risk, but the greatest risk is not accepting one.

There are also ways to be a spiritual companion on life's journey, but these ways are less job related and more based on counseling practices. Just being aware that they exist is a good place to begin. However, they may require more formal education then a person may have at present.

These works are instructing, advising, consoling, comforting, forgiving, and bearing wrongs patiently. These deal with more emotional needs and needs of the spirit. That is why they may take formal preparation prior to an intervention. But simple things like tutoring someone to read, discussing life choices from an unbiased standpoint, extending empathy and sympathy, forgiving others for inappropriate remarks or actions, and overlooking minor mistakes, are all things each of us can do right now in order to make the world a better place.

Working with others is not easy, and doing the right thing takes skill and patience. Too often people assume that they know what needs to be done, but seldom is that the best or most productive approach. The saying slow and steady wins the race can apply to our dealings with people as well. Knowing what to do is as important as doing it. Caution needs to be taken in not over extending ourselves and/or not smothering the recipient with too much care and concern. It is a fine line, and we must not forget that a little can and does go a long way in offering both care and support.

Be gentle, supportive, patient, and compassionate when offering help. A nudge sometimes works much better than a push and lasts longer. By being there, traveling and journeying with a person, staying present and focused, a person in need of your gifts may be less fearful and more accepting. Remember, a person in need usually did not get this way overnight, and will not do a complete turnaround overnight. Focus on the habit of Going the Extra Mile for the process and not necessarily the long term outcome. It takes time to change attitudes and actions. See yourself as a catalyst for positive change and then leave the rest up to the Universe for the final long term result.

Recall, too, that prayer is an action. You can always remember someone positively in your daily prayers. Research indicates that when people who are ill are prayed for, they heal faster. And those people who pray for others do not have to know the recipient at all. Prayer is a method of Going the Extra Mile that can help anyone anonymously and those doing the praying are the better for it. As has been stated, what goes around comes around. In Going the Extra Mile, the doer needs to start off on the right foot for achieving positive outcomes.

Napoleon Hill's Self-Confidence Formula

Going the Extra Mile is so important for self-actualization and fulfillment that Dr. Hill authored a self-confidence formula that is critical in conditioning the mind. This formula for self-confidence aids in acquiring whatever you desire in life. It is suggested that this formula be printed off and placed in locations where it can be read and reread. For example, the bathroom mirror is a good place to start. Upon awakening in the morning and before retiring in the evening, the formula can be read and allowed to seep down into the subconscious mind. Below is the formula as Dr. Hill wrote it in *Think and Grow Rich*:

First: I know that I have the ability to achieve the object of my definite purpose in life; therefore, I demand of myself persistent, continuous action toward its attainment, and I here and now promise to render such action.

Second: I realize the dominating thoughts of my mind will eventually reproduce themselves in outward, physical action, and gradually transform themselves into physical reality; therefore, I will concentrate my thoughts for thirty minutes daily, upon the task of thinking of the person I intend to become, thereby creating in my mind a clear mental picture.

Third: I know through the principle of autosuggestion, any desire that I persistently hold in my mind will eventually seek expression through some practical means of attaining the object back of it; therefore, I will devote ten minutes daily to demanding of myself the development of self-confidence.

Fourth: I have clearly written down a description of my definite chief aim in life, and I will never stop trying until I shall have developed sufficient self-confidence for its attainment.

Fifth: I fully realize that no wealth or position can long endure, unless built upon truth and justice; therefore, I will engage in no transaction which does not benefit all whom it affects. I will succeed by attracting to myself the forces I wish to use, and the cooperation of other people. I will induce others to serve me, because of my willingness to serve others. I will eliminate hatred, envy, jealousy, selfishness, and cynicism, by developing love for all humanity, because I know that a negative attitude toward others can never bring me success. I will cause others to believe in me, because I will believe in them, and in myself. I will sign my name to this formula, commit it to memory, and repeat it aloud once a day, with full faith that it will gradually influence my thoughts and actions so that I will become a self-reliant, and successful person.

Signed: _____ Date: _____

As you read and then reread this success formula, notice how much of its application relies on Going the Extra Mile. In the fifth paragraph, Dr. Hill clearly states that this formula works because it is a law of nature. Our thoughts bring about the construction or destruction of our lives. The impulses of thought have a tendency to clothe themselves in their physical equivalent, states Dr. Hill. This is so important that it might be described as one of the basic commandments of life. Irish author John O'Donohue adds: "Every single thing is somehow the expression and incarnation of a thought. If a thing had never been thought, it could never be."

Absolutely, it is worth your time and effort to read, recite, review, and memorize this formula because it helps to establish self-confidence and works toward conditioning your outcome in life by facilitating your actions in the here and now.

By improving myself, I improve the world. By desiring the achievement of my definite major goal in life, I set high standards for myself and everyone involved. By Going the Extra Mile, I draw my dream closer and closer to reality in the physical plane. Step into your future, by doing it now!

Right now, today, this very moment, begin to go the extra mile. Keep yourself in motion and advancing toward your desire by giving yourself to others in order to create a better life for all.

I know for a fact that when I go the extra mile, I feel better because of it. Little thoughts that come to mind with the imperative of *Do It Now!* give me a sense of fulfillment and gratitude for having done so.

Those who read the Bible believe that the key to happiness is gratitude for the riches that life has given us. In order to be grateful, we must notice things. Books on gratitude, journals on gratitude, movies on gratitude, songs on gratitude, practices on gratitude, affirmations on gratitude, meditations on gratitude, and beliefs on gratitude all abound.

Meister Eckhart states: "If the only prayer you ever say in your entire life is thank you, it will be enough." When you are Going the Extra Mile you are paying it forward and saying "Thank You" to life. You are confidently stepping into a realm where you create the outcome by your actions.

Words are important, but action is the cement that holds the words in place. Actions speak louder than words because actions are concrete, and words can be ephemeral and abstract. Blend the two, and you have a prize winning recipe for fulfillment. "I love you" sounds very romantic, but unless it is fulfilled in action no real commitment is there.

Think of those people who go or have gone the extra mile on your behalf. Could you imagine life without them? Parents, teachers, mentors, employers, wives, husbands, friends and family, who for whatever reason found you worthy of their extended benevolence. These individuals are irreplaceable in your life and create those timeless memories that never leave us.

A word, a gesture, a smile, a compliment, a helping hand, time spent together, time spent in silence, all add up to someone giving because it filled a need. In my life this has happened many times, and I am grateful for it. These messages delivered by others cause a person to pause and reflect on the trajectory of their lives. It could be a turning point, a starting point, an end point, a point of departure, or simply a moment in time that is never forgotten. No matter how it occurred, our lives are the better for it.

This is cause for gratitude because without these divine intrusions in our lives, the outcome may not have been as positive. Gratefully extend a heartfelt "Thank You" to the Universe for placing these people in our path who took the personal initiative to go the extra mile. In the end, when we revisit and consider the path our life has taken it may just have been one of these selfless souls who altered our course for the better.

Likewise, you may just be that messenger of goodness in someone else's life today. Don't ignore the push to get the job down. You just might be the angel unawares.

Below is an excerpt from Irish author John O'Donohue's book *Anam Cara.* It speaks to the human desire to make our works visible through expressing ourselves in various ways. One way to do this is by choosing to go the extra mile. He writes:

The human deeply desires expression. One of the most beautiful ways the soul is present is through thought. Thoughts are the forms of the soul's inner swiftness. In a certain sense, there is nothing in the world as swift as a thought. It can fly any-where and be with anyone. Our feelings too can move swiftly; yet even though they are precious to our own identity, thoughts and feelings still remain largely invisible. In order to feel real, we need to bring that inner invisible world to expres-sion. Every life needs the possibility of expression.

When we perform an action, the invisible within us finds a form and comes to expression. Therefore, our work should be the place where the soul can enjoy becoming visible and present. The rich unknown, reserved and precious within us, can emerge into visible form. Our nature longs deeply for the possibility of expression in what we call work.

Philosophical in content, O'Donohue's remarks state in a more spiritual manner what Napoleon Hill believes to be the process and benefits of Going the Extra Mile. Thoughts turned into action make the invisible real. This personal expression of thought is manifested in Going the Extra Mile for all to see.

Story Time

Question: What are some ways thoughts can be turned into action?

Answer: Often it is difficult to quiet our mind, and during meditation thoughts continually crop up that seem to sabotage our progress. This is referred to as the Monkey Mind because like a monkey our thoughts dart everywhere and are seemingly out of control. The idea is to capture these thoughts and focus on them one at a time. Pick a thought that involves Going the Extra Mile and follow it through to completion. Perhaps someone you know is experiencing hardship and has put up a Go Fund Me page. You consider making a donation but this was a passing thought and you never followed up. If on the other hand, you captured that thought and followed through, you can put that thought to rest and proceed to the next item. Remember slow and steady wins the race!

In my life I am content if I can address one or two concerns a day that need fulfillment. At the end of a month, these tally up to 30–60 plus actions taken beyond the normal to do list. Looking back that is quite an accomplishment by anyone's standards. Progress not perfection. Inch by inch it's a cinch.

Do It Now!

Begin right here, right now, by doing these activities.

1. What things are stirring within you as you consider more of what you can do in Going the Extra Mile?
2. Target one or two areas wherein you feel called to make a difference.
3. Write out opportunities that you have for Going the Extra Mile in these areas.
4. Do one or two of these actions today. Note the results.
5. Reread this chapter highlighting words, phrases, or sentences that are significant to you.
6. Review the Twelve Riches of Life. Rank the Twelve Riches highest to lowest as they have significance for you. 1 being the highest and 12 the lowest.

Instead of working on your highest ones, consider working on the ones more toward the bottom of your list. This is where you will experience your greatest growth.

7. Before falling asleep, think of the things that happened today. Express your appreciation to the Universe for all the good you gave to others and all the good others gave to you.

8. Read, post, and memorize the Self-Confidence Formula.

*The question isn't who is going to let me;
it's who is going to stop me.*
—AYN RAND

The Channel of Giving

Giving is a form of expression and giving is living.
—Napoleon Hill

*You have absolute control over but one thing,
and that is your thoughts. This is the most significant
and inspiring of all facts known to man! It reflects
man's divine nature. This divine prerogative is the sole
means by which you may control your own destiny.*
—Napoleon Hill

When there is a kink in a garden hose, the flow of water abruptly stops. Likewise, when you stop freely giving, you put a stop to the good that could invariably come to you. Negativity is this kink because it literally prevents us from receiving the positive outcomes that positive actions cause to happen. In order to restore the process, you must focus on what can be done for others by Going the Extra Mile.

Jewish author, Viktor E. Frankl, in his book *Yes To Life In Spite of Everything* asks: "What has come through to us from the past? Two things: everything depends on the individual human being, regardless of how small a number of like-minded people there is, and everything depends on each person, through action and not mere words, creatively making the meaning of life a reality in his or her own being. Therefore, we must counter the negative propaganda of recent times, the propaganda of 'Non-Sense,' of 'Non-Meaning,' with another propaganda that must be, firstly, individual and, secondly, active. Only then can it be positive."

Frankl wrote in German and was a prisoner in the concentration camps for several years. He survived the holocaust although most of his family did not.

In his writings Frankl is stating that it takes two things to make a difference: being an individual and being active. Saying yes to life is the integral key to becoming a positive person who can and does make a difference. Would not the principle of Going the Extra Mile fall under these guidelines? We are our best selves when we are individuals who can make a unique contribution to our lives and the lives of others. And, we do this by being active in the things that promote life and living. When we go the extra mile we are putting our best foot forward in action oriented steps. This journey ends in a life well lived.

As in any occupation, things work best with a toolkit for better job performance. In journeying from where you are today to where you desire to be, using the tools of the trade help you reach your destination more quickly.

You have been introduced to The Twelve Riches of Life, the Self-Confidence Formula, Q1 + Q2 + MA = C equation, the conscious and subconscious minds, gratitude, faith, the Big Four Principles: Definiteness of Purpose, Mastermind Alliance, Going the Extra Mile, and Applied Faith, negative and positive thoughts, words, journaling, affirmations, meditation or reflection, and most importantly taking action.

Each of these concepts is a tool in your Positive Mental Attitude Success Toolkit. You can use them separately or in combination, and they will hasten your journey. As you prepare to succeed in life, these concepts and more will prepare you for quicker and better outcomes. Practice does make perfect and in creating new habits, you are conditioning your mind for success. Let's discuss a few of the tools below. Hopefully, you will adapt and adopt them today and use them frequently to sharpen your success saw so to speak.

Affirmations

Let's begin with positive self-talk or affirmations. Affirmations are ways to colorize your mind toward positive outcomes. They are short declarative statements that you create for yourself in the present sense. When repeated over and over again they become a saying or mantra that is accepted by your subconscious mind as reality—whether it is or not. That's why they must be written and stated in the present tense, not in the past or future tenses, because your subconscious mind accepts literally what you tell it. Focusing on the past or the future will bring about no current results because the subconscious mind delivers what you tell it when you tell it. If you want success now, you must state it, believe it, and accept it as current fact. In this manner you will be preparing your subconscious mind to deliver what you are certain you already have. Examples are:

- My thoughts, words, and actions are always positive.
- My mind is clear, focused, and peaceful.
- All good things easily come to me.
- I use my thoughts to attain my highest good.
- I achieve my burning desire.
- I am filled with all the energy, wisdom, and love the Universe provides.
- I am treated fairly and with respect because I treat others the same way.
- I find the good in all things.
- Success and abundance are mine.
- I seek only my good and good for others.

You get the idea. Start by reading the statements over several times daily. Commit some to memory. Next, write four to five affirmations of your own for each area of your life such as work, family, friends, desires, health, goals, etc. Make them short, to the point, positive, and in the present tense. Read them out loud several times a day, upon waking up and going to sleep. As you condition your mind to always default to positive thinking, you become what you think about most of the time according to William James. Dr. Hill says it this way: "What the mind can conceive and believe, the mind can achieve."

Use affirmations daily to work to positivize your mind in a gentle, peaceful way. Awaken your five senses by purposefully experiencing something positive each day. Listen to classical music, pet a purring cat and linger with your touch, take time to experience what you are eating and enjoy the flavor of the peach, apple, or pear one tasteful bite at a time, really look at a flower appreciating the color, shape, size, design, and contrast it embodies. Next, smell the flower's unique fragrance. Inhale the aroma and excite your sense of smell.

By seeing, hearing, tasting, touching, and smelling, you can send positive messages to your subconscious mind as you enjoy beauty daily in the here and now. Sooner or later your subconscious mind will send back to you messages that are hints, ideas, insights, intuitive feelings and answers that will assist you on your journey if you pay attention to them. By seeing yourself living your best life with a positive mental attitude you will begin to condition your mind to bring about what you desire in the here and now.

Gratitude
Next, let's turn to gratitude.

When we focus on the things small and large that we are grateful for, we bring more of those things into our lives. When we go to sleep, counting things that we are grateful for works much better than counting sheep. Little things do mean a lot, and your list of ten things that you are thankful for daily could resemble mine below. Remember, when you express gratitude for what you already have, you create a chain reaction of goodwill customized by your Positive Mental Attitude. My list reads:

- I am grateful for my pets because they bring me companionship.
- I am grateful for today's good weather because it makes my commute to work easier.
- I am grateful for friends and family because staying in touch brings joy to my day.
- I am grateful for tomatoes because they are healthy and tasty.
- I am grateful for the aroma of my morning coffee because it wakes me up.
- I am grateful for the home I live in because it provides me with many comforts that are available to me.
- I am grateful for my ability to read because when staying at home I can become an armchair traveler.
- I am grateful for my work because it provides me with an income as well as the ability to make a contribution.
- I am grateful to be alive because of the many things that I have yet to experience and accomplish.

I recently made a list of things that I enjoyed on vacation, although all was not perfect. It amazed me to recall the many good things that brought me joy and happiness during my time away. And, it also reminded me that by focusing on the good things, many of the not-so-good things pale in comparison. When we compliment rather than criticize, we look for things to be happy about and at the same time make the inconveniences, set-backs, upsets, and not-so-positive happenings less significant. These things did happen, but they do not overwhelm us if we remember what went right and brought us joy.

Negativity, worrying, fault finding, complaining, and criticism are all downward spirals that lead us to a place of annoyance and sadness. Why go there? Stay on the sunny side of the street and remember the good times and forget the bad.

We cannot go wrong if we follow the advice of Albert Schweitzer, who stated: "Example is not the main thing in influencing others. It is the only thing." If we only focus on the positive and do things for others in a positive manner, we align ourselves as well with the good things that the Universe has to offer.

Journaling

Keeping a journal helps you to document the progress that you are making. It can also contribute to breakthrough revelations as to what may be causing you to stay stuck in one place. You can use prompts in your journaling that focus on a certain subject, or you can just write extemporaneously for ten to fifteen minutes in the morning regarding what is on your mind at the time. Journaling helps you extract ideas from your experiences and gets these ideas down on paper and out of your mind. It is therapeutic because once written down, you are free to forget about the issues that were brewing in your mind and clogging your thinking.

Over time, journaling helps you to see patterns in your day by day activities. It helps you to record what it is you are thinking in comparison/contrast to what it is you are doing. Journals are written for you and not for other readers. Grammar, spelling, formatting, are all insignificant because you will not be judged or graded on these things. The important thing is to write non-stop in order to drain or siphon off ideas and concerns that may have been festering over time. These issues could delay your progress and prevent you from reaching your goals. Uncovering these things helps you to recognize them, to move past them, and in time to eliminate them altogether.

Journals do not have to be expensive. They can consist of loose leaf pages in a three ring binder, an economical notebook, or a bound book. It is best to use something that lays flat because you do not want to become encumbered by tools that are annoying to use. A pen that writes smooth and easily across the page is what I prefer because it accommodates my thought process. Other people prefer pencils because they believe lead is a good conduit for thoughts, but I prefer a fine tip flair pen. Each to his own.

Drawing can be added to your journal as well, or diagrams, or word maps—whatever suits you. Just be certain that the journal is a place for you to record your thoughts at the moment. After a period of time, two weeks or a month, you might like to reread what you have written and see if there is any pattern. Do certain themes reappear? Do worries carryover from day to day? Or, do they become resolved? Do desires stay the same, or are they the flavor of the day?

Reviewing what you have written can give you insights that you may not have noticed before. Journaling can bring your subconscious mind into the forefront. Dreams may come up that awaken new ways of thinking and unmask old problems.

Journaling can and does create a conduit for better performance now because of renewed focus on what is meaningful and helpful to you. Give this tool a chance. Don't take it for granted. It will not disappoint you in the long run.

Note cards

Another way of keeping track and positioning yourself in the present are simple note cards. I use this technique daily. At the top, I place the date, year, and day of the week. And then I add numbers as items occur down the left hand side of the card. I use 5 x 8 cards because they provide me with the extra space I need. Day by day, week by week, month by month, I file these cards in a box so that when needed I can simply thumb through them and see if I have done something. These comprise my daily to do list.

I began this process years ago, and it works for keeping me organized. When I am doing something else such as journaling, praying or meditating, a thought frequently occurs that I do not want to forget. Previously, I would stop whatever I was doing and attend to it. This broke my concentration, but I did not want to forget the thought. Now, instead, I keep my note card at the ready and when a thought disrupts my concentration, I jot it down. There it is. Not forgotten and in place when I need it. This technique placates my mind, and assures me that whatever it is that was so important is now on the card to read when I am finished.

My daily card can include bills to be paid, appointments, reminders for upcoming services, pet medications, phone calls to be returned, servicing of vehicles, and on and on. This works for me in relieving my mind of the trivia that sometimes controls us. And, it provides peace of mind in knowing that I can always review the cards when and if I may have forgotten anything.

I have taken several workshops in Colorado from Dr. Clarissa Pinkola Estes, the author of *Women Who Run with the Wolves*. In one session she indicated that she wrote the entire book on note cards in fifteen minute intervals because that was the time she had available.

Isn't it amazing to think that a classic book celebrating twenty-five years in print could be authored on simple note cards? There must be power in this technique. Right then and there I decided to use the tool. If it works, use it. Right? I also use note cards for other things such as gratitude lists, etc., but I mentioned my daily use because it helps to free up my mind from the mundane things that demand so much of our focus. Try it for a month and see if it makes a difference in your positive mental attitude.

Meditation—Reflection—Praying

Whatever you call it, going within to that still, silent, personal space of spirit has long term benefits. Frequently removing ourselves from the daily stress and activities associated with day to day living causes us to reboot and return energized to our exterior lives. I am a reader and I like to reflect on what I have read. Reading for me connects me to the ages and brings all humanity together as a continuum of inspiration. Without the printed word, our heritage from our ancestors and others would be lost. On any given day, I can read Shakespeare, Napoleon Hill, King Solomon, Ayn Rand, St. Teresa, Dickens, Emily Dickinson, Lincoln, and on and on. Authors from past and present can present their cogent ideas for our reflection and even meditation.

By reading autobiographies and biographies we can get inside a person's thinking and gain new understanding as to what their chief aim in life was and how this enabled them to make an everlasting contribution. Hawkins, Nightingale, Kennedy, and numerous others with a passion for living overcame their adversities to make a difference for all of us. We definitely stand on their broad shoulders and owe them a heartfelt Thank You for each of their contributions to mankind.

Simply by remembering why we celebrate the lives of individuals enables us to appreciate why we are here on this planet and what we may contribute. This can and does encourage us to think beyond the normal, everyday happenings in our lives and to look toward a more improved future for the human race.

There are many styles of prayer as well. Too often prayers are prayers of petition—asking the Universe, God, the Higher Power, or whatever name your prefer, to give us something. It has been stated that these are not necessarily the best types of prayers to use. Rather, prayers of gratitude for what we have been given are found to be more effective. By saying "Thank You" instead of "Please Give Me" we are already acknowledging all that we have and are grateful for in life. You can come to your own conclusion as to which is better by trying both approaches and comparing the results.

Additionally, I like to read about ordinary people who have begun special movements in the world that may have promoted radical changes. Whether it is St. Francis of Assisi, Martin Luther, Martin Luther King, Jr., John Wesley, Dorothy Day, Mother Teresa, John F. Kennedy and so on, each is remembered for what they gave, not for what they took. Their lives continue to inspire and direct us yet today.

Using *meditation, reflection* and *prayer* can provide you with personal insight and help you uncover your purpose in life. Start slowly. Ten to twenty minutes a day is enough. Afterwards, jot down any feelings or realizations that you may have had in your daily journal. Consider these two quotes on prayer as you open your mind to the process.

> *"Whatsoever we beg of God, let us also work for it."*
> —JEREMY SCOTT

> *"Your greatest power lies in the power of prayer."*
> —W. CLEMENT STONE

Negative and Positive Thoughts

Napoleon Hill began his classic work *Think and Grow Rich* with the chapter heading: Thoughts Are Things. He goes on to state:

> Truly, "thoughts are things," and powerful things at that, when they are mixed with definiteness of purpose, persistence, and a burning desire for their translation into riches, or other material objects.

Thoughts can be either negative or positive as well. Actualized thoughts can harm or heal just as words can do. It is imperative to control our thoughts for positive outcomes if that is our goal. Negative thoughts compete with positive thoughts minute by minute, hour by hour, day by day, and can and do determine our outcome in life. If we want positive results we must control our thoughts.

Thoughts are abstract and things are tangible. Equating thoughts with things seems inappropriate at first. Consider that thoughts produce things, and everything springs from a seed of thought. Therein you begin to understand the significance of beginning with the right thoughts for the best outcomes. It is like putting your best foot forward. A negative thought, a misstep, can lead to a wrong destination. A seed of thought is like an apple seed. If you want an apple tree as your result, you must plant this seed and not one that produces a tomato.

People have tried counting their positive and negative thoughts. This tally assures us that our thoughts are in competition with each other much like the good and bad angels that are pictured on opposite shoulders in some picture books. Recognizing this is important, but more important is controlling the direction that our thoughts take.

Stopping negative thinking in its tracks should be the goal, not measuring which occurs more often. Negative thoughts can be stopped by first recognizing the thought, and then switching gears by stating STOP and substituting a positive thought replacement.

I have seen people wearing rubber bands on their wrist, and whenever a negative thought occurs they snap the rubber band on their wrist once as punishment. This only works if a negative thought is then replaced with a positive one and rewarded. Hopefully, this practice will not be needed for too long.

In teaching classes on Positive Mental Attitude, I have students list ten things they cannot do beginning with the words "I can't . . ." For example:

I can't fly an airplane.

I can't stay awake past 10 p.m.

I can't become a gourmet cook.

I can't lose weight.

I can't learn geometry.

I can't achieve my goal.

I can't stay healthy.

I can't keep my house clean.

I can't drive a stick shift.

I can't go the extra mile.

Next, they are instructed to read their list out loud to a partner by each taking turns. Reading these lists, the students are solemn and thoughtful and read with a seriousness in their voice as if their "cannots" were set in stone and personal commandments.

Then I have them substitute the words "I can" for "I can't" and have them reread the list to one another. Immediately, their moods change. They giggle and even laugh. Very soon they connect with their personal power and became self-actualizing individuals. In this moment they realize that they are the ones in control.

One student in a parenting class said it all by summing up her feelings. Initially, she stated in her own manner of speaking "I can't find me a boyfriend."

When spoken out loud, her voice was sad and forlorn. She was the victim, not the victor. Next, when her turn came again she stated, "I can find me a boyfriend."

By raising her awareness with this new, positive statement she affirmed, "I can't find me a boyfriend, and I don't want me one either!" Revelation. She put herself in the driver's seat and got a hand clapping ovation! There is power in words both positive and negative. Consider the poem by Ella Wheeler Wilcox. Ask yourself if your self-talk harms or heals your life.

You Can Never Tell

You can never tell when you send a word
Like an arrow shot from a bow
By an archer blind, be it cruel or kind,
Just where it will chance to go.
It may pierce the breast of your dearest friend,
Tipped with its poison or balm;
To a stranger's heart in life's great mart
It may carry its pain or its calm.

You never can tell when you do an act
Just what the result will be,
But with every deed you are sowing a seed,
Though its harvest you may not see.
Each kindly act is an acorn dropped
In God's productive soil;
Though you may not know, yet the tree shall grow
And shelter the brows that toil.

You never can tell what your thoughts will do
In bringing you hate or love,
For thoughts are things, and their airy wings
Are swifter than carrier doves.
They follow the law of the universe—
Each thing must create its kind,
And they speed o'er the track to bring you back
Whatever went out from your mind.

The Big Four Principles

Definiteness of Purpose, Mastermind Alliance, Going the Extra Mile and Applied Faith are the Big Four Principles that work as cornerstones for the Science of Success System. Each principle works independently, but utilized together they form a powerhouse of strength that cannot be defeated. Each principle is unique and requires additional understanding in order to incorporate it into Dr. Hill's research and refined teachings. But united, these four principles combine and the positive end result is greater than the sum of the parts.

This alchemy works as if by magic to bring your definite major purpose into your personal world sooner rather than later. The best way to make this happen is to follow the suggestions religiously step by step and be open to insights and inspiration that will lead you to the results that you seek. Timely hints that you recognize from the Universe awaken your creativity and inspiration and allow you to better focus on the end result that you are seeking. Remain alert. Be aware. Be patient. Be proactive. Most importantly be an action person who goes the extra mile while expecting positive results from the Universe as due compensation for the effort that you have put forth. Consider the quotation by Eleanor Roosevelt:

> You gain strength, courage, and confidence by every experience in which you really stop to look fear in the face. You are able to say to yourself, "I lived through this horror. I can take the next thing that comes along." You must do the thing you think you cannot do.

Begin now by doing "the thing you think you cannot do" for both yourself and others.

Story Time

Question: How do I unintentionally stop the giving process in my life?

Answer: Entitlement can stop the giving process in a person's life. By seeing yourself as the recipient rather than the giver you create expectations for yourself that reverse the natural flow of the river of life. When you expect, demand, force, or simply feel that people should do for you regardless of what you have done for them, you go against the Laws of Nature. It can begin by taking things for granted, not saying "Thank You," and always expecting more to follow what has already been given. Finally, demanding that this is done is the last straw when dealing with a person who has this sense of entitlement. This process can proceed on course for some time, but eventually the source will dry up and discontinue the service. The goal for each and every person should be empowerment and not entitlement. This can be learned on a sliding scale, but for some the lesson is never understood. Remember, if you feel as if you are being taken advantage of you probably are. If this is the case, stop Going the Extra Mile for the person in question and move to help someone who appreciates the effort that you are making. Sooner or later they will find another to take advantage of, and you will be off the hook and the better for it. Sounds harsh, but tough love can be.

Do It Now!

Begin right here, right now, by doing these activities.
1. Itemize the success tools in your tool kit. How are you using and benefiting from each one?
2. What is your favorite tool? What is your least favorite?
3. Which one works to your greatest advantage? How so?
4. Are there others not mentioned that you find helpful? For example, if images inspire you, try creating a picture collage regarding ways to go the extra mile. By assembling these images and

reflecting upon them, you may be inspired to take action.

5. If music is something that also promotes the feeling of Going the Extra Mile, consider creating a playlist that you listen to frequently. Songs such as "Wind Beneath My Wings" is one that relates the benefits of Going the Extra Mile.

6. Reread this chapter highlighting words, phrases, or sentences that are significant to you.

7. Before falling asleep, think of the things that happened today. Express your appreciation to the Universe for all the good you gave to others and all the good others gave to you.

Light tomorrow with today.
—Elizabeth Barrett Browning

Chapter 6

The Companions on the Journey

*A kindly word here, a kindly deed there,
a pleasant smile everywhere, and this world
would be a better place for all mankind.*
—NAPOLEON HILL

*The master mind principle is a method of applying
the assets of others to whatever end you may wish to
pursue through a mutually beneficial association.*
—NAPOLEON HILL

Together we can accomplish more. Teamwork makes the dream work. For where two or three are gathered together in my name, there am I in the midst of them. All the thought starters together point to cultivating the principle of the Master Mind Alliance while working on Going the Extra Mile. Benefits untold evolve from creating companions to accompany us on the journey of life. The easiest way to begin is by Going the Extra Mile. Giving before getting involves forethought and planning. But, the benefits gained prove beyond a doubt the reward of laying the groundwork in advance.

Repeatedly people stop the flow of giving by not wanting to go the extra mile, or even the first mile. This stops nature in its tracks because in order to receive a surplus you must first plant the seed.

The world today by anyone's standards is a different one. People are loners, looking for a leader who will sweep in and save the day. Responsibility is a thing of the past. Commitments are short term. Friendships dissolve overnight due to petty disagreements. Apologies and the mending of fences are unheard of in our society. People react instead of connect. Instead of listening for understanding, opinions become the hard and fast rule without any thought to authenticity. Stubbornness prevents relationships from forming and being right is more important than getting along.

One way to begin to break this cycle is by Going the Extra Mile. It is the little things that mean a lot, and when this is recognized and acted upon, the world begins to change with one act of service at a time. By anticipating or seeing a need and filling it, the process is jumpstarted and people begin to understand that a community that works together is more productive than a person who wants to go it alone.

Literally a shift in understanding is required. It takes effort, discipline, and persistence, but the long term results are worth it. Ever drive in a foreign country where the driving pattern and the position of the driver are different? Many complain that the drivers in the designated country are driving on the wrong side of the road and seated in the wrong side of the car.

If you drive in another country, Ireland for example, immediately you are required to see things differently. Your attention shifts, your posture shifts, your eyesight expands, different rules of the road increase your learning curve, and your awareness is heightened. Just from driving a vehicle that many of us have driven most of our adult lives.

Now, just consider what interacting with others who are not in your home, family, social circle, work environment, state, country, etc., can do for the exponential growth of your world. Remember the basic motives in life? Well, these motives can easily be turned around and become our basic fears and excuses not to act.

Dr. Hill says that you must have these basic motives in your life or you have not learned to live very well. He states: "You will find that unless specific goals of your life, no matter how small, are supported with a proper number of these motives, you are not going to be interested in carrying out those plans to a successful conclusion."

Most importantly, Dr. Hill adds, "The more of these basic motives that you have urging you on, the more likely you are to get in touch with the subconscious mind and draw on the power of *Infinite Intelligence.*" When these basic motives are denied or overlooked or used as mechanisms of fear you will not progress.

A good exercise is to take each of the basic motives at face value and decide, here and now, to go the extra mile by doing something that supports the desire to become actively involved by simply Going the Extra Mile. You are hereby priming the pump in the hope that more good things will follow. Consider this list:

1. **Desire for self-preservation**: Today, look beyond yourself, and your time here on the planet and consider your legacy. What can you do right now that will merit recognition when you are gone? It does not have to be announced to the world. The Universe knows. Do a good deed. Plant a tree. Feed an animal. Sponsor a student. Donate an hour to a cause. Write a note. Give a token gift.

2. **Emotion of love**: Tell someone today that you love them. Consider the ramifications of that one statement. Friends or family will appreciate this as you initiate or end a conversation.

3. **Emotion of fear**: Face a fear that you have. Fear of the dark. Fear of old age. Fear of loss of income. Confront it. Turn out the lights. Acknowledge your age and physical changes. Spend less. Choose one fear and overcome it.

4. **Emotion of sex**: Cultivate friends of either sex. Socialize when you would rather not and learn about others.

5. **Desire for life after death**: Study the spirituality of leaving. Consider and discuss what may happen beyond this life. Meditate, reflect, and pray. Volunteer at a hospice.

6. **Desire for freedom of body and mind**: Support inclusion rather than exclusion. Find commonalities rather than differences. Accentuate the positive while eliminating the negative.

7. **Desire for revenge**: Get over it. Apologize. Move on. Carry no hurt or hate with you to tomorrow. The burden you carry is just not worth the extra weight!

8. **Emotion of hate**: Understand righteous indignation and support causes that erase the hate and violence in society. Do something against human trafficking for example. Buy fewer products and reuse and repurpose more. Ask what little things you can do to make a small yet significant difference. Step lightly on this planet and work to lighten your personal footprint.

9. **Desire for self-expression and recognition**: Participate when asked. Express your talents and awareness through service to others. Share a story, write an essay, and discuss values and beliefs. By preferring not to share or express yourself, you are erasing yourself right out of memory and existence. Give what you can of yourself, right now, in the here and now.

10. **Desire for material gain**: Do the work that creates a life of meaning and financial security. Develop your potential in an area where you have a gift. Do the thing you love, and you will never work a day in your life. This is your gift to the world.

Considering the relationship Going the Extra Mile has to the other principles of this philosophy is of significant importance. Dr. Hill states, "You will be surprised how easy it will be to obtain cooperation from others when you follow the habit of Going the Extra Mile. The mental attitude you show when you go the extra mile will cause others to help you."

Be reminded that thoughts are contagious. States of mind are contagious. Mental states that are negative might be compared to diseases that are contagious. These states may be likened to diseases of the mind. The cure is to keep your mind positive. Rely on your higher self to combat the negativity that is present and give it a dose of the only vaccine that will work. A positive mental attitude.

We know that history repeats itself, and looking back to 1932 and the presidency of Franklin Delano Roosevelt, we remember a similar state to what we are encountering today. Thought patterns, images, and stories that focused on the good that was happening rather than the bad were needed to put the United States of America in a better frame of mind. Reading what was done then causes one to wonder if a similar program conscientiously put in place might do the work of turning around the face of the nation.

By replacing fear with faith, Roosevelt's administration saved a nation. The thrust of the program was working together in harmony in a spirit of faith in order to promote a single objective. Here is what was done. Consider the steps and assess what is not working now, but if changed could work productively in our future.

Napoleon Hill relates this plan as follows:

First. Both houses of the Congress worked together in harmony for the first time. Under the magnetic personality of the new President who inspired their confidence, a majority of the members of the Congress momentarily forgot their party lines and put their collective shoulders to the wheel to pull the nation out of the sloughs of depression.

Second. Many of the newspaper publishers of the nation were called together in a conference and asked to replace the scare headlines they were using with headlines which would show some hope and promise and the possibility of a brighter future for America. Instead of playing up business failures, they were asked to accent business successes. Human interest stories were to point up those who had remained valiant and who had kept their heads above water.

Third. Operators of radio stations were asked if they would cooperate and have their commentators and news editors say something pleasant instead of continually painting the darkest, gloomiest aspect of events. For some reason, the average person loves to hear about misery and trouble, poverty and want, disaster and peril. And in the early thirties the newspapers and the radio reflected this negative thinking until it because a vicious cycle, one supporting the other, so that it was almost impossible to put over a positive idea.

Fourth. Religious groups, disregarding denominational differences, got behind the movement and worked together to promote positive, hopeful thinking.

Fifth. The leaders of both major political parties supported the administration. We are not talking about the rank and file; we are talking about the leaders. May it be said to their credit, they got behind Franklin D. Roosevelt, Republican and Democrat alike. If they had not, the fear stampede would not have been stopped and there would not have been a restoration of confidence in the short time in which it was achieved.

Sixth. As overwhelming majority of the people, forgetting political and religious beliefs, rallied behind President Roosevelt and supplied the impetus and popular acceptance necessary to bring success to the President's program.

In order to turn the tide toward recovery for a nation reeling in bad news, fears had to be relinquished and the thinking of the entire country had to be reversed. This was accomplished with good news stories, the promotion of developing a positive mental attitude, self-reliance, the benefit of taking personal action through work at home and on the job. Such concepts as victory gardens in every home, recipes that utilized rations for better nutrition, the sacredness and wholesomeness of pulling yourself up by your bootstraps, all contributed to the healing of a nation.

As Roosevelt used fireside radio chats to condition Americans to the image of an improved future, he talked the nation out of a longer depression one American at a time. The concepts of personal initiative, building a better self-image, focusing on all things positive, teamwork, and collaboration with the government's back to work program all contributed to healing and improved conditions.

Do you sense a similar need now? Considering the state of the nation today and its people, would a similar, well integrated and supportive plan work? The key is in like-minded focus and harmony for individuals working toward a common, positive objective. If we can agree to disagree and move forward with what is important to everyone, the plan can begin to bring healing to a nation that is still reeling from one world crises after another and health concerns that affect us all.

Where to start? It's obvious. Start by Going the Extra Mile for yourself, next with your friends and family, and then your local communities to intentionally promote healthy, one small act consciously done for the promotion of good.

This can and does create a wellspring of events that can turn the tide toward all the good things that are taking place, rather than the bad. Start now, start today, and do the thing and you will have the power.

I was given a coffee cup years ago by a high school student's mother who worked in our teachers' cafeteria. I defended her son and his abilities while in the checkout line, and the mother overheard me. Not knowing she was his mother, she thanked me for seeing the good in her son privately the next day and gave me the coffee cup. It appropriately reads:

New Beginnings
Each day is a new beginning . . .
another chance
to learn more about ourselves,
to care more about others,
to laugh more than we did,
to accomplish more than we thought we could,
to be more than we were before.

I have never forgotten that gesture from the mother who wanted to hear a word of encouragement about her son rather than bad reports and criticism about his behavior. I still have the coffee cup!

Story Time
Question: Do you have a memory of something someone did for you in recognition of a good deed you did for them?

Answer: Surprises are one of the things that fill our lives with joy and gratitude. By nature, surprises are unexpected and sometimes spontaneous. The really good ones we keep to ourselves and treasure them over time—a personal memory that is to be cherished. Ones we share are those that speak to the heart as well but are more public.

Flowers given are usual tokens of surprise. Whether for special occasions such as graduations, birthdays, or just because, they linger in our thoughts long after the blooms have faded. Once as a little girl, my daughter ran ahead of me on a walking path and returned with a handful of someone's blooming lilacs. The gesture was a positive one, but the source could have been better chosen. I accepted them with a feeling of pride because of her thoughtfulness, but then I had to share a lesson about someone else's personal property. Bittersweet, but nevertheless remembered fondly.

As a second job, my father ran a used car business in front of our property with the help of my brother. Friday was auction day and one or more cars usually arrived at home on Friday afternoons. Seeing me outside the house, my father asked me to accompany him to one of the cars that had just arrived. This car was nothing special, so I did not know why he wanted me to see it. Usually, it was my part-time job to detail the cars, so I figured that was on his agenda. This time was different. He walked me up to the car, asked me to look inside, and accompanying the car home from the auction was a mother cat and her kittens. I was appropriately excited and pleased. Knowing my love for cats, this will always be a special, private moment that my father shared with me. I am glad to this day that he surprised me instead of telling me what was in the backseat before I had a chance to see for myself. Sharing moments with someone and lingering over good times are one of the best gifts in life.

Do It Now!

Begin right here, right now, by doing these activities.

1. What are the basic motives that jumpstart you into action?

2. Which ones especially cause you to get moving into action right now? This is the extra success ingredient that will advance you toward your goals more quickly.

3. Recall a special gift someone gave to you in appreciation for something you had done for them. How does this memory make you feel?

4. Reread this chapter highlighting words, phrases, or sentences that are significant to you.

5. Considering the crises the world is in today, what one thing can you do to assist in making the world a kinder, gentler, more positive place for all? Are you doing it?

6. When making memories with others, what type of things will you do differently now than you have done before? Why so?

7. Before falling asleep, think of the things that happened today. Express your gratitude for all the good you gave to others and all the good others gave to you.

It's time to start living the life you've imagined.
—Henry James

The Discovery of Mission

*The principle of Going the Extra Mile is the
master strategy of the entire philosophy,
for it gets action. It is the active principle.*
—NAPOLEON HILL

*If anyone doubts the existence of Infinite Intelligence,
that person need only study the stars and planets,
and the precision with which they are related to
one another, to become convinced of Its existence.*
—NAPOLEON HILL

How does *Going the Extra Mile* aid us in discovering our mission or purpose in life? Why are we here? What are we meant to do? Are we really making a difference for ourselves and others? How do we know for certain that this is the path we are meant to be on? What happens next, and next, and next. . . ?

Discovering what we are meant to do in life takes time and reflection. Looking within ourselves in order to recognize our unique gifts and talents, causes most people concern because it is a spiritual process that resembles mining our soul. In today's society, less and less time is found daily for self-discovery and analysis. That is exactly why it is important to take the time and to do it, regardless of what else you might be missing. Because what you are "missing" is much less important than what you will find. Given time to recognize what makes us happy, what brings life to the daily grind, and what makes our souls smile, is worth more than hurrying through the checkout lines. Pause frequently and ask yourself what is stirring within you. Why do certain thoughts bubble up and create mental ripples in your thinking? Could these recurrent thoughts possibly lead you to what you are put on this planet to accomplish? Your life's purpose, your mission, your definite major purpose? It is worth considering?

Turning seventy-two in June, 2022, I often wonder what work I have to finish in this life. I am a connector, a teacher, a mentor and would like to think of myself as an agent working for *Infinite Intelligence.* I enjoy bringing people and experiences together for the good of the whole. When someone experiences something that helps them have a smoother day or more profound life, it makes me happy. We all like to hear that we have made a difference, and by being a person who matches people with what might help them gain a foothold, I see my purpose. I guess that my job has not been completed yet because I am still here doing what I have done in order to help others move toward their definite major purpose. I wonder where this gift is leading me, and wherever it happens to be I will show up.

Little things open up the Universe for me. Help that shows up when needed, the companionship of my animals, the note, phone call or conversation that is right on the money for what I felt I needed in the moment. Less worry and more living. The ability to complete things with ease rather than with dread. Connecting with someone who knows how you may be feeling and helping to direct your path. Sunshine, nature, opportunities that arise out of nowhere, and the courage to continue on without giving in to anxiety or even depression.

Daily things to be grateful for in life. Little things that God created that bring pleasure like good food, a good night's sleep, no pain, good health, and people to interact with that are likeminded. All these things speak to me of the Divine. Miracles would be nice, but do not have to be out of the realm of ordinary. Eyes to see, ears to hear, and optimum use of the senses can fill a person with joy. I guess I would have to say my greatest connection to *Infinite Intelligence* occurs due to my use of being open to the Spirit. I try to relate to daily happenings that point a finger toward *Infinite Intelligence.* Simple and profound at the same time. Take away these things and life would hold less joy and more difficulty. We can be blessed in many ways and the simple gifts are oftentimes the very best.

Oftentimes, only in retrospect do I see God's involvement in my life. As events occur like family gatherings involving marriages, births, deaths, and other occasions it seems that the journey of life is a march forward, but only in hindsight do I see God's hand in things.

Being creatures operating in time, prayer seems to be a way to look ahead in anticipation of where we hope to be and/or are headed, and reflection seems to aid us in knowing that God is with us in good times and bad.

For me, it seems that God "snaps" in and out of my life although I know that this is my perspective and that God is always there. Obviously we are contained within God, not vice versa. We live and move and have our being as a part of God, not distinct and apart from the Creator.

I like to think of God as a loving Father, even a Daddy, who listens to our requests and then already knows what is best for us. Good parents intend no harm to their children, and likewise God wants what is best for us even if we do not realize it or understand it ourselves.

I do not recall a single peak experience of God in my life. I sense a closeness and a caring and direction as I listen to the still, small voice within, but I would have to say my closeness to God occurs when I recognize a sort of grace or help that I know for certain was not of my own doing. It is a moment of realization that a prayer has been answered, or a time to take the next step without fear or trepidation.

I seek out more information on spirituality now from qualified individuals whom I believe are walking ahead of me on the path to eternity. Just petitioning, attending church, reading the Bible and spiritual works, is not always enough. Rather I look for modeling of the principles that are being taught and endorsed. I like to align myself with doers because I feel that they are growing God's kingdom for the good of the whole and not simply their personal interests.

So, people who demonstrate the principles in action are those who speak to me. I like reading the lives of the saints in order to see what they did, not in a suffering manner, but in a teaching manner, to bring Christ into the lives of others. This is never easy because inside we all have the critic who badgers us with the thought that all of this may be meaningless and a waste of time. However, if learning, witnessing, and modeling Christian attitudes and ways of being improves my life and assists in making me a better person, I am for it. Being positive and open helps us look toward the light and turn our back on the darkness.

There is too much of the "dark side" in today's society, and attempting to change it for everyone might be futile, but we can begin with ourselves and change it for one and that makes a difference at least for me. Can't necessarily save the world, but we surely can improve our own life by seeing the good that exists in creation.

When I study anything intricate, I see God in the picture. The human body, nature, birth, death, and the cycle of life causes me to consider the why and wherefore of it all. I pray and sometimes become frustrated with myself because I perceive little positive movement in my life. I set goals only to sometimes push them back. I ask the usual questions and seem to get different responses to the same questions. I do know that if I keep busy, remain a seeker, and look for answers to life's questions, I feel better and accomplish more.

God speaks to me indirectly daily with an inner knowing. Sometimes I simply ask God, "What do you want me to do next?" when I am overwhelmed and cannot see beyond the problem to a solution. Through patience and persistence I generally find an answer. I like to see progress rather than envision it. When something needs doing it bothers me until it is done.

Setbacks don't always produce the kind of comeback that I may be seeking, however I know that failures cause us to rethink, retool, reengage, and restore our lives to an acceptable equilibrium and beyond. God is the God of the present. Living in the past or future holds no promise. It is only in the eternal now that we can work on our purpose and hopefully by figuratively holding God's hand, He will lead us to the outcome that He foresaw when we were knitted in our mother's womb.

My view of what companionship is has developed over the past months. The process, if it is one, involves intense listening and praying for and with a person for increased personal awareness and life support. Spiritual companionship is not about becoming closer to God, but closer to those who are strangers, neighbors, friends, and family—and therein we also become closer to God. By taking the back road, God leads us to Him on a less traveled path.

Spiritual companioning is about learning and somewhat internalizing another person's story, needs, and direction in life—whether or not it is our own choice. It involves acute listening so that another's life story is honored with an attempt to understanding what may in the past have eluded them or us. It is remaining open to where the Spirit may direct us and could lead us. Both lives are enriched and renewed through spiritual companioning. It is not enough for one to undertake a relationship without the intent of expanding both people in the process. We listen, we consider, we grow, and we renew our own lives also in this process in guiding and championing another.

In being companioned by someone, I have found new areas of approach and interest that beforehand I may not have considered. I have shared moments of my life's concerns as well as have listened to another's, and it shows a pattern and a purpose in all lives that is undeniable. Being on the same road as another individual helps a person perceive what may be coming and understand better what has happened in the past. Next, a future orientation that is fresh and new is always another option rather than what was or might have been. Being able to acknowledge mistakes and certain tendencies helps a companion better understand the universality of the human condition.

Not much has changed over the years, but when that is encountered and realized, everything can and does change. Being better able to pray to God in many forms and formats enriches our prayer experience and eases the tension of just doing it the "right way" or one certain way. Studying the various traditions helps a person acknowledge where their own tendencies occur as well as expanding their overall perceptions of what else is available to use for expansion and change. There is no one right way to do a single task—multiple ways can help a person reach the desired outcome.

Sitting and talking and primarily listening aids both the "giver" and the "receiver." It feels good on both accounts and enables a person to offer themselves in silent or real dialogue with each other that can aid in softening the load, promote renewal, and even transformation. Just by paying attention and focusing, a person can begin to see and realize that the outer world and our inner world are truly part and parcel of the same whole. One always impacts the other. By sharing, we progress and open up new avenues of enrichment, caring, and perception.

I like the prayer written by Thomas Merton. He was a monk living in Kentucky. It reads:

"My Lord God, I have no idea where I am going. I do not see the road ahead of me. I cannot know for certain where it will end. Nor do I really know myself, and the fact that I think that I am following your will does not mean that I am actually doing so.

But I believe that the desire to please you does in fact please you. And I hope I have that desire in all that I am doing. I hope that I will never do anything apart from that desire. And I know that if I do this you will lead me by the right road, though I may know nothing about it. Therefore will I trust you always, though I may seem to be lost and in the shadow of death. I will not fear, for you are ever with me, and you will never leave me to face my perils alone."

Story Time

Question: Does God or *Infinite Intelligence* really care about us?

Answer: I for one believe that God is present in our daily lives. When a person is open to signs and signals, *Infinite Intelligence* does relate to us in personalized ways. Be alert. Be aware. Ask for direction and guidance. Follow your intuition and remain open to thoughts, ideas, suggestions, and random happenings that serve to "connect the dots" of your life. Spend some time reflecting on the timeline of your life and jot down major happenings. Look for circumstances that seemingly appeared out of nowhere that helped direct your path. This can be done over a period of time, but the idea is to reflect on how you arrived at where you are today. Over time, you may begin to see patterns that have brought you to this point.

Often happenings that seem to be interventions from above are referred to as coincidences. My friend from Mexico has labeled these occurrences "Dios-cidencias." In other words, they are not just random happenings, but interventions by God in our lives. I like the thought. Author Squire D. Rushnell refers to these interventions as GodWinks. When they happen to us, we know their authenticity without a doubt and accept this gift of overwhelming grace. What may seem of little merit to others when retold, has major importance to us because we can connect the dots. For many of us the Heavens open up, and our immediate response is "Thank You, God." Could be God Going the Extra Mile!

Do It Now!

Begin right here, right now, by doing the activities below.

1. Our time, our talent, and our treasure are three ways of making a contribution to the world. Which one do you use most frequently?

2. If you mainly give from your treasure (money), why not try giving from your time and talent?

3. Recall a special gift of time someone gave to you. How did you respond to this gift?

4. Perhaps someone taught you a skill, instructed you in a process they were familiar with, or engaged you in their favorite hobby. How did you respond to this gift?

5. Recall a special gift of treasure someone gave to you. How did you respond to this gift?

6. In conjunction with the three means of giving, have you ever experienced any GodWinks in your life? Jot them down. How do you explain them and their significance to you then and to you now?

7. Considering the crises the world is in today, what one thing can you do to assist in making the world a kinder, gentler, more positive place for all? Are you doing it?

8. Before falling asleep, think of the things that happened today. Express your appreciation to the Universe for all the good you gave to others and all the good others gave to you.

A dream doesn't become reality through magic,
it takes sweat, determination and hard work.
—COLIN POWELL

Chapter 8

The Purpose of Work

*You know, work is a liaison office between
our desires and their fulfillment.*
—NAPOLEON HILL

*You either take possession of your mind and direct
it toward the attainment of your major definite purpose,
or your mind will take possession of you and give
you whatever the circumstances of life hand out.*
—NAPOLEON HILL

You may be wondering what the purpose of work has
to do with Going the Extra Mile. It is a good question to consider, as when discussing definiteness of
purpose, your life's mission, your heart's desire, Dr.
Hill discusses the nature of work. Putting a plan into
action takes personal initiative, persistence, and a
strong desire to reach our chosen objective.

Considering this, Dr. Hill differentiates between
drifters and non-drifters in his terminology. This distinction alone can help students clarify and understand why some people remain stuck. Perhaps they

can then begin to understand why, too, they are not meeting their objectives in life.

Drifters are those individuals who do not think for themselves, accept the thoughts, ideas and opinions of others, and acts upon them as if they were their own.

Characteristics of Drifters:
- Followers
- Take the line of least resistance
- Repeat same mistakes
- Have no definite major purpose or plan in life
- Do not practice self-discipline
- Know no difference between positive and negative thinking
- Follow stray thoughts that drift in and out of their minds
- Seldom, if ever, go the extra mile
- Display no personal initiative

Non-Drifters are individuals who think their own thoughts and assume full responsibility for them, whether or not these thoughts are right or wrong.

Characteristics of Non-Drifters:
- Leaders
- Have a definite major purpose
- Formulate a definite plan to attain this purpose
- Take action to carry out the plan to attain this purpose

- Learn from their mistakes
- Practice Going the Extra Mile
- Move on their own personal initiative
- Maintain a positive mental attitude
- Take pride in personal achievement
- Keep their mind on the things they want and off the things they do not want

The above characteristics of drifters and non-drifters point to what contributes to their success or failure in life. As a person begins to analyze why some people succeed and others fail, he begins to understand that there is a system of success that favors the student of life who learns the principles and puts them to active use.

Together, Napoleon Hill and W. Clement Stone crafted the *Science of Success Educational Manual* during their collaborative time together. This volume details the 17 Success Principles researched by Dr. Hill, and also has developed into a semester long course with one week of intense study devoted to each principle.

Suffice it to say, this text is the culmination of Dr. Hill's lifelong work in one comprehensive volume of thought. I read it as the bible of self-help material because everything emanates from it. Nowhere is there a more precise explanation with historical examples than in this work.

Initially, it was used in courses conducted in prisons in the Chicago region, but today it is taught throughout the world. The *Philosophy of Success* as discovered and shared by Dr. Hill is given to students anxious for a concrete step by step analysis and application of what determines success in a person's life and how to create it for any individual ready to accept the challenge.

Given the fact that *Think and Grow Rich* by Dr. Hill is the unmitigated success manual for its time and beyond, The Science of Success Course taught in affiliation with the Napoleon Hill Foundation today, is the key that unlocks the door for many on their journey to personal achievement. As a student, I myself have taken the course three times and benefited greatly each time I enrolled for the course. Its teachings and methods stay with you for a lifetime.

Sometimes, end notes on life—often called a person's legacy—can inspire others to emulate their actions. These recollections serve to bring a sense of pride and completion to a life well lived. Two recent deaths of an actor and an actress do provide food for thought on what can contribute to this type of performance in living.

Actor Sydney Poitier states that his mother's lesson of always remembering to say "Please" and "Thank You" opened doors in his career that otherwise would have remained closed. Such a simple lesson in living, but one most people never practice today because they feel the practice is old-fashioned and the results are inconsequential. Mr. Poitier proved otherwise. He explains: "A good deed here, a good deed there, a good thought here, a good comment there, all added up to my career in one way or another." Truly, it is the little things that add up to big results in life.

Another stellar actress and animal advocate is Betty White. She showed her love for animals by working seventy plus years in their care and funding. Although her career was in acting, her passion was demonstrated in her lifelong compassion for animals. She used her occupation to purposefully assist in whatever she could do to promote awareness of the needs of animals. Ms. White states: "My mother and dad were big animal lovers, too. I just don't know how I would have lived without animals around me. I'm fascinated by them—both domestic pets and the wild community. They just are the most interesting things in the world to me, and its made such a difference in my lifetime." Knowingly in another quote she states: "Kindness and consideration of somebody besides yourself—I think that keeps you feeling young. I really do."

And in relationship to having a definite major purpose in life, Betty White explains: "I always wanted to be a zookeeper when I was growing up, and I've wound up a zookeeper! I've been working with the Los Angeles Zoo for forty-five years! I'm the luckiest old broad on two feet because my life is divided absolutely in half—half animals and half show business. You can't ask for better than two things you love the most."

Consider the longevity of Sydney Poitier and Betty White. Both actor and actress were well respected and often acclaimed the best in their field. This did not happen haphazardly or without effort in their lives. They each had a plan and a purpose for their lives, and worked to complete that plan. Dr. Hill states: "If you will organize your time efficiently and relate yourself to others harmoniously, you may have anything you desire—provided you know exactly what you want, and are determined to get it." Both Poitier and White knew this reality in their beautiful lives and utilized their time consciously by creating daily habits that led to their preferred outcomes.

Viktor Frankl in *Yes to Life* writes:

Certainly, our life, in terms of the biological, the physical, is transitory in nature. Nothing of it survives—and yet how much remains! What remains of it, what will remain of us, what can outlast us, is what we have achieved during our existence that continues to have an effect, transcending us and extending beyond us. The effectiveness of our life becomes incorporeal and in that way it resembles radium, whose physical form is also, during the course of its "lifetime" (and radioactive materials are known to have a limited lifetime) increasingly converted into radiation energy, never to return to materiality. What we "radiate" into the world, the "waves" that emanate from our being, that is what will remain of us when our being itself has long since passed away.

It is not by chance that Betty White became lovingly labeled America's grandmother and Sydney Poitier became an early heartthrob for many in the middle decades of the Twentieth Century. People admired not only their talent but their desire to help others by Going the Extra Mile. They created standards of living that others could aspire towards. Their gifts were presented in doing for others and in the way they lived their lives.

It has been said that imitation is the greatest form of flattery, and may these two stars rest in the knowledge that their lives had merit beyond their own comfort.

Consider the quote by Charles H. Spurgeon: "A good character is the best tombstone. Those who loved you and were helped by you will remember you when forget-me-nots have withered. Carve your name on hearts, not on marble." It goes without saying that Poitier and White have indeed carved their names on our hearts.

If Going the Extra Mile for others is work, why do we do it? The answer is simply that both the giver and the recipient benefit in the giving and receiving process. It takes creative effort and ingenuity to come up with ways of Going the Extra Mile that are not stagnant, repetitive, lackluster, and do overs.

How is a freshness maintained and boredom averted in finding new avenues of approach? The answer could begin for each of us by Going the Extra Mile for ourselves as well as others. Taking care of ourselves before others gives a person a feeling of competence and ability to share. Something that is lacking cannot be shared, a pump that is not primed cannot produce water, and giving from lack and not plenty does not produce the desired outcome.

When flying, adults are asked in an emergency to put their oxygen masks on first before aiding others. Likewise in giving, treat your neighbor as you would like to be treated yourself and you will get the idea. Perhaps at night, mentally ask yourself what was done for you by others that made your day a better one. Perhaps someone brought you a cup of coffee, sat down to listen to you without glancing at their phone, offered to help with a project, called to check up on you, responded to an email with a positive compliment, offered to care for a pet when you are away, left a written note with a positive message for you to find, picked up your mail when you were traveling, jumpstarted your vehicle when the battery was dead, accompanied you on a trip in order to keep you alert while driving, plowed your driveway, remembered you with a gift on your birthday, walked your dog, and on and on. Sometimes, just by acknowledging the good things that occurred in your daily life, you can get ideas on how to be of service to others. It has been said that imitation is the sincerest form of flattery, and it costs us nothing to use it.

Things that people did for me recently that made me smile and were helpful as well were: picked up my Christmas Turkey from work and stored it in the freezer until I was back on the job to claim it, pushed my garbage can to the road so that I did not miss a weekly pickup while away, gave permission for me to use their artwork free of charge in a monthly publication that I was working on, asked me "what's for dinner?" in order to remind me to eat healthy, checked in on me to ask about the weather in my area, commented on a display that I did and added that many people stopped by to view it and enjoyed it, left notecards and containers at my home because the person recognized that I like to use these daily, and the heartfelt gift of a small change purse illustrated by one of my favorite artists was given as a thank you for favors rendered. Wow. All these things were done recently for me and were very much appreciated. Now, I have additional ideas of my own that I can use for others.

Another way of reminding ourselves of the benefit of showing kindness by Going the Extra Mile is a favorite of mine. I like to collect quotations that inspire me to action. I write these down and read them like affirmations. In that manner, they condition my thinking and eventually seep into my subconscious awareness. Here are some quotes on Going the Extra Mile. You can use these and add more of your favorites as well.

*Life's most persistent and nagging question is
"What are you doing for others?"*
—MARTIN LUTHER KING JR.

*Those best parts of a good life: little, nameless,
unremembered acts of kindness and love.*
—WILLIAM WORDSWORTH

*I've learned that people will forget what you said,
people will forget what you did, but people will
never forget how you made them feel.*
—MAYA ANGELOU

*Too often we underestimate the power of a touch,
a smile, a kind word, a listening ear, an honest
compliment, or the smallest act of caring, all of
which have the potential to turn a life around.*
—LEO BUSCAGLIA

*Perhaps you will forget tomorrow the
kind words you say today, but the recipient
may cherish them over a lifetime.*
—DALE CARNEGIE

*So many gods, so many creeds,
So many paths that wind and wind,
While just the art of being kind
Is all the sad world needs.*
—ELLA WHEELER WILCOX

When you are kind to others, it not only
changes you, it changes the world.
—HAROLD KUSHNER

Do all the good you can. By all the means you can. In all the
ways you can. In all the places you can. At all the times you
can. To all the people you can. As long as ever you can.
—JOHN WESLEY

The smallest act of kindness is worth
more than the grandest intention.
—OSCAR WILDE

No one has even become poor by giving.
—ANNE FRANK

The world is changed by your example, not by your opinion.
—PAULO COELHO

There are no traffic jams when you go the extra mile.
—KENNETH MCFARLAND

You cannot do a kindness too soon,
for you never know how soon it will be too late.
—RALPH WALDO EMERSON

Do your little bit of good where you are; it's those little
bits of good put together that overwhelm the world.
—DESMOND TUTU

We should give as we would receive: cheerfully,
quickly, and without hesitation; for there is not
grace in a benefit that sticks to the fingers.
—Seneca

How far that little candle throws his beams!
So shines a good deed in a naughty world.
—William Shakespeare

The best way to get favors is to start handing out favors.
—Napoleon Hill

Do It Now!

After reading and reflecting on the above quotations, make a list of several things that you would like people to do for you.

Consider that if you would like these things done for you, others would probably like them done for themselves too. Turn the tide and begin today by giving what you would like to receive to others. Finally, sit back and note the results. I believe that you will truly experience that saying "what goes around comes around" in a good way.

As you work with these concepts, it is important to remember that the significance in the lessons lies in the action taken afterwards. By taking action on what makes sense to you now, you are building your skillset one principle at a time. Studying the principles of success takes time. *Reading, relating, assimilating,* and *applying* the ideas that you are now studying in your daily life is the process that makes the critical difference and causes the outcomes that you want to happen in your life. Knowledge is not power. Applied knowledge is power. Just begin here and now to take one single step at a time to do the thing that your reading and reflection have inspired you to do.

Since this book is all about the principle of Going the Extra Mile and its benefits to yourself and others, here is where to begin. Start now by living out the images in your mind where you take action on what it is you intend to do. Only you know where your talents and abilities are and how they best serve the community in which you work and live, so get busy now in making a difference—a big difference by Going the Extra Mile right now, today, this very minute, and be the beginning of the transformation process that is waiting for you and your personal contribution.

One last suggestion. Before words and language, evolving man used images that he created in his mind's eye to foresee creatively the outcome that he was seeking. By mentally walking through the process in a series of corresponding images, man was mentally preparing himself for a successful outcome that corresponded to a series of events that he would undertake. By creating these mental images he could imagine himself successful in the hunt, around the campfire, enjoying the bounty of his catch, and witnessing to the fact that planning and visualization does aid positively in the outcome.

Today you can do the same. Whether you refer to it as daydreaming, visualization, focusing on the future, seeing tomorrow today, or just allowing your mind to create waking images of the end result you seek, you are conditioning your mind for success while giving your subconscious mind the message of what you want.

Story Time

Question: Does creative visioning do more than simply daydreaming?

Answer: Here is a quick story of how this worked in my life. For a few years, after having seen a breed of dog in Alaska that I liked, I decided that it was to be my husband's next companion in life. After all, I am an avowed cat person, but my husband who was on medical leave, needed a friend while I was at work. I asked people on the streets in Alaska what kind of dog it was, and the reply was "It's a Leonberger."

Never having heard of this breed, I did some research, and mentioned that I wanted a Leonberger puppy to my niece who lived in Alaska at the time. She replied, "Auntie, I looked, and they do not have those dogs here." I countered with, "But, I saw several and I know they have them."

Keeping the thought in the back of my mind for over a year, I began researching the breed and looking for breeders. People told me that the dog was too big, drooled, had a heavy coat, and would eat too much. Nevertheless, I still thought about the dog. During this time my husband was on leave from work due to medical reasons. We would commute to Texas for his cancer treatments frequently, and drove many times in order to have a vehicle while there.

On one trip, stopping overnight, we went down to breakfast in the elevator and when the door opened standing on the other side was a man with a Leonberger puppy. Immediately I said, "That's a Leonberger, right?" Next, I added jealously, "I hate you. Where did you get it?" He responded, "I just picked it up from a breeder in Indiana."

I could not believe what I just heard. How is this possible? I am on my way to Houston, stop for an overnight stay, and to find out from a stranger that what I was looking for was back home in Indiana after all. I asked if he could share the information with me, and he said that he would leave the breeder's card for me at the desk when he checked out. He did.

My husband Bob sighed because he knew it was all over from then on out. Getting back home to Indiana, I contacted the breeder, set up a meeting, and Lena came into my life in 2016. She was one of eight puppies and we had the pick of the litter because we were on a long waiting list. She will be six years old on March 19, 2022. We picked her up in May, 2016 and my husband died in August, 2016. Coincidence? I think not.

Lena is now my homeland security dog, travels with me everywhere, provides me with safety and company, and in reality I believe is the personification of my Guardian Angel. She came at just the right time, in just the right manner, for just the right reason when I needed her the most. A chance occurrence, synchronicity, or just plain luck? I believe all of the above. My subconscious mind never gave up on finding her and drawing her to me, and I immediately knew it was meant to be when that elevator door opened and the puppy appeared.

I for one am a firm believer in the power of work, and the workings of the subconscious mind. Hold those images of your desires in your mind's eye as if they are holy and sacred. Sooner or later you will draw to you what you envision the most at just the right time. Conceive it. Believe it. Achieve it. The ABC's of Success—only backwards. But you can pay it forward once you know the secret formula for creating images of those heartfelt desires in your mind's eye! Wisely, Dr. Hill states: "Everything one needs or desires has a way of showing up as soon as one is ready for it."

Do It Now!

Begin right here, right now, by doing the activities below.

1. Consider how you are progressing daily by Going the Extra Mile. Notice the benefits of this process. Record your thoughts in your journal.

2. How is the one principle of Going the Extra Mile causing your journey to take shape? Pause and reflect on how the other 16 success principles might cause you to progress even further in your journey. Consider the list below:

Definiteness of Purpose

Master Mind Alliance

Applied Faith

Going the Extra Mile

Pleasing Personality

Personal Initiative

Positive Mental Attitude

Enthusiasm

Self-Discipline

Accurate Thinking

Controlled Attention

Teamwork

Learning from Adversity and Defeat

Creative Vision

Maintenance of Sound Health

Budgeting Time and Money

Cosmic Habitforce

3. Review the characteristics of *drifters* and *non-drifters*. Can you forego being a *non-drifter?* How so?

4. Write a short prayer to *Infinite Intelligence*. Remember prayers of gratitude work better than prayers of petition. Recite it out loud.

5. Before falling asleep, think of the things that happened today. Express your gratitude for all the good you gave to others and all the good others gave to you.

The only person you are destined to
become is the person you decide to be.
—RALPH WALDO EMERSON

Chapter 9

The "To Do" List that Matters

A little job well done is the first step towards a bigger one.
—Napoleon Hill

*Have your mind continually open to
the reception of Infinite Intelligence.*
—Napoleon Hill

Each of us have different to do lists that we tackle daily either in mental or physical form. Most items on these lists are obligations that need our attention such as domestic chores, appointments, meetings, maintenance of vehicles, and on and on. Thinking back to my early years, I might question what was of significance that really mattered on my youthful to do list. It was education and all its ramifications. I mean both formal education and informal education as well as life experience.

One of the greatest gifts my mother gave to me excluding life was the ability to read. It seems understood in our day and age that people read, but worldwide there are still illiterate pockets of people who lack this skill. Let me entertain you for a bit regarding why I think reading is so important, and why globally we must make the effort with each new generation to make certain reading is of primary importance in each and every child's life.

Why read?

I believe that the greatest educational gift of all time is the ability to read. From earliest instruction, whether at home or at school, our ability to decipher meaning from marks on a surface opens up new and exciting worlds for everyone. Once the association between written characters and another's thoughts is established, there is no holding anyone back.

Just think about the excursions one takes by reading. We can visit ancient civilizations, future extra-terrestrial homes, deep caverns hidden inside the Earth, and all things real and/or imaginable. Reading transports us across time—to the past, to the present, and even eons into the future. Time becomes our benefactor as we read.

For every writer, the ability to share thoughts with others expands our years and allows people to communicate beyond the barrier of time. Think about any known person today—living or dead—and their contribution to our world. More often than not, it is retained through their writing that is read over and over again. A Shakespeare, a Dickens, an Einstein, the Bronte sisters, the great spiritual writers of the world, and on and on, all contribute their knowledge by sharing unique thoughts through the written word.

This can be a lot to take in, but it is 100 percent the key to living well now, and later even living beyond our earthly years.

How can you get started creating a lifelong reader in your family? Here are ten simple things you can do today to encourage the gift and joy of reading for yourself and others.

Use these self-starters as opportunities to practice Going the Extra Mile for yourself and others.

1. Model reading practices daily by encouraging your family to see you reading and prospering from it.

2. Read together and aloud. Read to your family and when age appropriate, have the children read back to you. Take turns reading a single page each. Help decipher words that are difficult, but never scold when a child hesitates. Just say the word and continue.

3. Use simple wordless picture books wherein you can create and read your own story. No books? Help children tear up old materials to create a page by page story that they "author" and read to you. Either before or after, you can continue to model the practice by creating something yourself in picture format. Use photographs, recipes, travel brochures, and old newspaper ads to construct your story. Create a "by" line. Make it official.

4. Record a short reading on the phone that children can play back and listen to as many times

as they want. Even better, if the book is handy they can follow along word by word. Later, you can have them read the story to you. Remember, they may have simply memorized the story and are not really "reading," but pretending is a good start that leads a child in the right direction.

5. Begin a saga about your family such as a made up story about "Lena, our Homeland Security Dog." Relate continuing stories that entertain and educate about what Lena does for the family day in and day out.

6. Ask your child to read a recipe to you as you prepare it. Help them to understand what the measurements mean and why using exact measurements is an important part of preparing a dish.

7. Research your culture and ethnic background with your child. Begin with upcoming holidays and significant days that are meaningful in your own upbringing. Educate your child as to why this is important as you read about the traditions that you celebrate.

8. Post a daily schedule and have your child see it, hear it, and read it if possible. If it is important to you, it will be important to them.

9. Read a poem, short fairy tale, a legend, or something pleasant each day before bedtime. Make it a ritual. If you forget, the child will ask for it no matter the age.

10. Buy books wherever and whenever you can afford them. The library is also a source, but helping a

child build a private book collection of their own will insure that reading, reflection, and repetition is taking place frequently and this always enhances learning.

Too many things to do? Just pick one idea today and add a new one every few days. The benefits will accumulate and soon you will begin to see why reading is the key to unlocking all the riches in life for your children. Reading is cumulative and contagious. The more you practice reading, the more your children will want to be involved. Repetition is the key in learning to read, and it is a key to lifelong success as well. Why not begin today in helping your child become an avid reader? As we are told, "If you can read, you can do anything." The truth. Plain and simple.

Story Time

Question: How does my mother's Going the Extra Mile connect with my passion for reading?

Answer: When I was in first grade my mother was told that I would be held back unless my reading improved. Shocked during the final parent/teacher conference my mother stated: "Why, she can read!" Once outside the classroom alone with my mother, she told me that I just preferred being read to and that was going to stop now. Not a teacher herself, but understanding the reading process better than the teacher, she outlined ways to essentially force me to read. Several of the practices are the ones I enumerated above.

Fast forward to eighth grade and my entrance exams for high school. When the results of the test were reported, I scored the highest in reading. For the next four years I was placed in Freshman 1—the highest track out of all 13. All because my mother knew the significance of reading beyond any doubt and was not about to allow her youngest child to become a non-reader. I had a parent who cared, and this made all the difference for me during my life. Anything can be learned by reading. By Going the Extra Mile in teaching me the benefits of reading, she provided me with the ability to tackle anything I set my mind to in life.

Do It Now!

Begin right here, right now, by doing the activities below.

1. Take time today to read for pleasure. What have you learned?

2. Want to become an authority in a field of study? Consistently read in that one area for thirty minutes a day. Soon, you will become knowledgeable enough to approach being an "authority" within three to five years if you continually pursue this practice. Why? Because you are setting yourself apart from those who do not read.

3. Read a bedtime story to a child. No child around? Read it to your inner child. You both will be the happier.
4. Write in your journal about books you enjoyed reading as a child. How did these books shape who you are today?
5. Read your personal prayer out loud.
6. Express gratitude before going to sleep for all the good that came to you during the day.

Strive not to be a success but rather to be of value.
—ALBERT EINSTEIN

Chapter 10

The Compensation of Giving

Get into the habit of Going the Extra Mile because of the pleasure you get out of it, and because of what it does to you.
—NAPOLEON HILL

You must do that for which you are paid to keep your job, but you have the privilege of rendering an overplus of service as a means of accumulating a reserve credit of good will which entitles you to higher pay and a better position.
—NAPOLEON HILL

For many people, focusing on finances can be detrimental to having a positive mental attitude. The idea of experiencing a loss can bring this about. Just watching the stock market this week take a nose dive puts many people into the depression era mood. If we allow it, we can succumb to these feelings almost spontaneously because what we think about we bring about. I am not negating the downturn at times in the economy and stock market. Rather, I am suggesting that our response to it creates our reality in the moment.

Dr. Napoleon Hill lived through the depression era and himself experienced many adversities in his investments and in his life. The difference in his outcome from many who experienced the same is that he never gave up. Losses in the market, failures in publishing, poor land investments, lack of harmony with his associates, trials in personal relationships, family issues regarding what his relatives thought that he should or shouldn't do, and criticisms regarding his chosen life's work all led to many setbacks. But, he persisted in his goal. He never crossed over the river of life to the negative side and ultimately that made the difference for his life's work and for each of us who are the recipients of his teachings.

Today, people say that his examples are dated, and that the historical references are not significant for our times. Those individuals are looking for a What's In It for Me Philosophy of Success at the onset, and fail to comprehend that the finances come as a footnote to life's real work. By Going the Extra Mile, a student of success braces for the slings and arrows in life, and never abandons the quest for a positive outcome.

Theodore Roosevelt stated at the Sorbonne in 1910:

It is not the critic who counts; not the man who points out how the strong man stumbles, or where the doer of deeds could have done them better. The credit belongs to the man who is actually in the arena, whose face is marred by dust and sweat and blood; who strives valiantly; who errs, and comes short again and again; because there is not effort without error and shortcoming; but who does actually strive to do the deeds; who knows the great enthusiasm, the great devotions; who spends himself in a worthy cause, who at the worst, if he fails, at least fails while daring greatly, so that his place shall never be with those cold and timid souls who know neither victory nor defeat.

At the beginning of this "lesson plan" for Going the Extra Mile, you were asked to begin to consider your definite major purpose in life. For many, this is hard to identify because primary, secondary, and university training do not teach us how to do this. During my numerous years of formal schooling, never once was I asked what it was that I wanted to do with my life, my brief time on this planet. I knew that I had to make a living, but that quest for my passion that gave me satisfaction, pleasure, and fulfillment never entered into the process. All I was told was that I had to figure out something to do within the context of my formal education in order to make a living but not necessarily a life. I was well prepared to graduate into the world and to get a job, but I was never taught about the process of attaining life's riches along the way. This was an aside, a diversion, a missed opportunity, or at best a hobby that might bring some satisfaction along the way. What salary I made became the litmus test of my success, and not the lives that I touched, the legacy that I was leaving, or the riches of life that came to me as secondary benefits.

As wisdom over time is acquired, our life's purpose becomes something we look back upon and wonder how we arrived where we are. One of the best courses in my university studies that I took three times was Dr. Hill's *Science of Success Course.* The first time that I took the class it was for non-credit. I had never taken a continuing education course in my life because I felt that this type of course would not merit my time and effort. However, since my mentor was teaching it, he asked me to consider taking it. Immediately, I felt that I was lacking something in his eyes because this, in my understanding, was a positive mental attitude course. And, if it was recommended to me, I thought that he was saying that I lacked this type of mental attitude. I took the course and studied the principles, and saw the wisdom in Dr. Hill's teachings. I went on to take the course two more times to gain further depth within each of the principles. Today, I review the materials frequently. When I am encountering an issue, I ask myself what principle of success I am failing to use. The answer always comes to me, and I can correct the problem by focusing on renewing my strength in the one or more principles that I am failing to apply.

By Going the Extra Mile initially and agreeing to study the material, I suspended my belief in a negative outcome. I met likeminded people who also wanted to broaden their understanding of success and how to achieve it. I then began to apply these principles, starting with Going the Extra Mile, in my daily life and I could see and measure the difference in the positive outcomes. I befriended people whom I would not have spoken to before and looked for common areas of agreement rather than differences. I created opportunities for Going the Extra Mile at home and at work, and encouraged my family members to do the same. I accepted challenges that formerly I would have turned down and was always better for taking the risks. I watched others and noticed how they too went the extra mile and saw the positive outcomes in their lives. By simply saying "yes" and then following through, I changed the course of my life for the better and the finances I accrued attest to my ability to make life better for myself and others. But, by beginning with others, you learn to see the good that you are capable of doing, and because they benefit you benefit too.

This past week, I drove to Chicago with a friend to pick up some artwork from David Lee Csicsko. He is the first cousin of a lifelong friend, and she introduced me to him years ago. David is a juried artist and creates modern images of saints among other things. These images are not typical, but they make you stop, look, and consider metaphorically what he has created and the message that he wants to deliver.

I am doing a display where I work on saints and relics and I thought that a mixture of current and historical art would cause visitors to stop and think. David has allowed me to display fifteen of his framed pieces for twelve weeks, and I am very excited to see the response. Both he and I have gone the extra mile with this project because I could have easily done something routine and safe. And David could have declined the invitation to allow his art to be displayed, but because of Going the Extra Mile we came together to accomplish something inspiring and unique. It is my hope that because of his depictions, visitors to the show will come away with new understanding and appreciation of the lives of the saints and perhaps model some of their characteristics in their own lives.

By chance, I am working with another Chicago artist, a photographer, through his wife, Pat Cowan. Pat's husband Ralph was an innovative photographer who traveled the world in pursuing his passion to capture images that created his life's work. He died on February 9, 2006, and Pat decided that she wanted his legacy to live on through another organization. In 2021 she donated his photographs to the organization I currently work for as Assistant Archivist. I was asked to act as curator for this donation, and I am pleased to say that a show of his work is currently at MoonTree Studios on campus. Art needs to be seen in order to make a difference in the lives of ourselves and others. By viewing what people are passionate about in their own lives, we can begin to see how and where we can pursue our definite major purpose as well.

For more than twenty years, I have worked and traveled with Don Green, the CEO/Executive Director of the Napoleon Hill Foundation in Wise, Virginia. Don is an art collector and invests in art from around the world. He does not create the paintings or artworks himself, but he promotes these works for others to view and appreciate. Some of the paintings from his collection have been donated to the University of Virginia's College at Wise, and he hopes that the students will be inspired to pursue their dreams and ambitions as well as their careers when they see these works from around the world.

Don likes to pursue his interests by investing in things that will bring about a profit that he in turn donates to a good cause. I can say that I among others have been the recipient of his generosity and many kindnesses. That's what leaving a legacy is about. Not the bottom line in your check book, but the goodness that you spread around when you could. This is Going the Extra Mile. It is risky and may not always benefit you immediately but years later when someone mentions to you something that you did, that glow of recognition warms both hearts.

So, financially, you can make a living by what you do, but you make a life by what you give. It takes finesse, contemplation, and execution of the intention to give, but the value is there for a lifetime.

How do you put yourself out there? By Going the Extra Mile. Make a difference for someone other than yourself. Consider the options. Do a little each day, and at month's end you have created a bushel basket full of generosity that spills over goodness into your life.

Another thing I recently experienced could happen to all of us. A father died and his family was the recipient of his collection of cultural items. Not having the same passion for his collection that the father had, the son decided to "gift" the items after a church service to anyone who was interested in taking one or two pieces in his father's memory. A little reception was held, the items were displayed, and people were invited to take what held interest for them. No strings attached. Just a desire to pay it forward.

So, can I take Going the Extra Mile to the bank and count it as one of my assets? In my opinion, it is your only asset that counts at the end of each lifetime. Lewis Carroll states: "One of the deep secrets of life is that all that is really worth the doing is what we do for others." Lord Byron states: "To have joy, one must share it."

What are you doing right now for others? How are you sharing the gift of yourself? The answers to these two questions will be recorded in the Universal records and will be the balance sheet that ultimately counts in the end. Are you currently operating in the red or in the black?

Story Time
Question: How does Going the Extra Mile by others inspire you to do the same?

Answer: Watching others go the extra mile brings opportunities for doing more of the same into the lives of others. Organizations such as United Way, various missions, and church sponsored events encourage people to be of service. Doing good in a positive mental attitude has a way of forecasting the future by promoting more good things to come. Expectations lead to actions, and actions lead to results. When I see people going beyond normal expectations and doing beneficial things, I am encouraged and inclined to follow in their footsteps. Be open for new ideas that may be to your liking. Inspiration surprises us by providing unique opportunities to make a difference. We may not be able to make the sun shine daily, but sometimes we can prevent more rain by having an umbrella handy for those in need.

Do It Now!

Begin right here, right now by doing the activities below.

1. Consider the Hindu Proverb:

   They who give have all things;
   they who withhold have nothing.

   How have you seen this work in your life and in the lives of others? How so?

2. Consider your unique talents and gifts. How can you use those to benefit others? How does this giving without expectation help you too?

3. Draw a map of your giving territory. How far does your little light shine today? How can you make it go further?

4. Consider how you might contribute to the larger world picture? What "war" do you want to fight?

5. Express gratitude before sleeping for all the good that you did today and all the good that was done to you.

6. Say your personal prayer out loud.

We cannot hold a torch to light another's
path without brightening our own.
—BEN SWEETLAND

The Habit of Gratitude

*Don't forget to express gratitude daily, by prayer
and affirmation, for the blessings you have.*
—NAPOLEON HILL

*A mind dominated by positive emotion, becomes a favorable
abode for the state of mind known as faith. A mind so
dominated may, at will, give the subconscious mind
instructions, which it will accept and act upon immediately.*
—NAPOLEON HILL

You might be asking yourself what *grace, gratitude,*
and *faith* have to do with Going the Extra Mile.
Well, my response would be just about everything.
These often unmerited and unasked for gifts from
the Universe are how Divine Intelligence assures
us that we are worthy because we are the sons and
daughters of our Heavenly Father, Infinite Intelligence, or the Force. Name it what you like, Dylan
Thomas describes it as "the force that through the
green tube drives the flower." Think about it. For
humans it might be the force that through our back-
bone drives our mission.

Sometimes termed GodWinks, coincidences, synchronicities, or divine pats on the back, these spiritual aids assist in propelling us forward as we pursue our mission in life. When we recognize that we have received this type of gift, we know it immediately. It is meant for us alone, and we understand its meaning intuitively. We may get the shivers, or our neck hairs may stand on end, but when this gift is received there is no doubt that it was meant for us and our well-being today and in the future.

Grace is something we do not earn, but yet are capable of receiving as a gift. Gratitude is something most of us understand, because at times in our lives we have been grateful for a helping hand, an unexpected gift, or anything of goodness that has been supplied to us. Faith is the knowing and in the believing in advance that goodness is real and something worthy.

There is a passage in the Bible that confuses many people when heard. Taken from the Gospel of Matthew it reads:

> "Whoever has will be given more, and he will have an abundance. Whoever does not have, even what he has will be taken from him."

Pondering this statement, it seems highly unfair—something like the "rich get richer and the poor get poorer." How could this be inspired writing when it seems to contradict what is stated elsewhere in the Gospels? Self-help writer Rhonda

Byrne believes that something is missing in the translation, and she suggests that the missing word is gratitude. Adding the word gratitude to the passage makes it read:

Whoever has gratitude *will be given more, and he will have an abundance. Whoever does not have* gratitude, *even what he has will be taken from him.*

Read in this way, it now makes sense given our study of Going the Extra Mile. Gratitude begets gratitude and those who give it receive it back many times over thus increasing their abundance. Those who fail to show gratitude have diminishing returns and become poorer and poorer in spirit.

In *A Christmas Carol* Charles Dickens relates this very story regarding Scrooge who is poor in spirit if not in finances. When he is visited on Christmas Eve by his deceased business partner Jacob Marley and the three spirits of Christmas Past, Christmas Present, and Christmas Yet to Come, Scrooge embarks on a spiritual journey regarding his insensitivity to others. His awareness is heightened and he realizes what a fool he was in focusing on external riches but lacking in the milk of human kindness. Gratitude for life, for family, for friends, for neighbors, for clients, for workers, and even towards himself never passed his lips or came out of his pockets. Instead, he turned inward and chose not to recognize the suffering of others right in his midst or even his own. But, through grace he awoke in time on Christmas Day to change the trajectory and thereby the final outcome of his life. Faith in the good that he could create in the lives of others less fortunate made the miserly Scrooge into Father Christmas. When this happened, gratitude was given to Scrooge for his positive contribution and he was able to drink the milk of human kindness for himself.

According to Wikipedia, grace is defined as the divine influence which operates in humans to regenerate and sanctify, to inspire virtuous impulses, and to impart strength to endure trial and resist temptation. It also states that grace is "the love and mercy given to us by God because God desires us to have it, not necessarily because of anything we have done to earn it."

For me, grace is the pleasantly unexpected intervention of God in our lives in a recognizable way. Humorously, it might look like a "get out of jail free card," or a happenstance, coincidence, synchronicity, or Godwink that a person can recognize and only be a gift unmerited, uncalled for, and unearned from God.

When and if these divine interventions occur, a person may have a knowing that a message and/or a gift has just been received from the Almighty that could produce goosebumps, an eerie recognition, a sensation, a mixing of the senses (synaesthesia), an internal emotional knowing, a spiritual stirring, or even just an "aha moment." Sounds crazy, right? But this postcard from the divine is received with joyful acceptance and the thought that possibly more nudges, taps on the shoulder, and/or gut reactions are God's way of telling us He loves us and cares for us in a heavenly Father/Mother manner.

I like the concept of *grace*. It is one of those gifts that keeps on giving because a person can replay the moment in their memory as an assurance that it did happen. It could be as simple as God bringing us a metaphorical cup of coffee to sooth our day or troubles, or it could be as big as a billboard message that is intended for everyone but touches our soul intimately due to the personalization of the message that only we would recognize. Grace can cause us to take a deep breath, exhale, and be assured that God has our back. When a person receives grace, he or she can be empowered by it. It sparks the divine light within us, and gives us a momentary respite from the aches and pains or slings and arrows that the world throws as us.

I have experienced moments of grace in my life, and some I only understood in retrospect. Looking back over my life's timeline I can identify Divine Intervention that occurred with only a glimpse of initial recognition. But, by looking back I can see God's grace there helping to direct my path. As my discernment matured, so did my understanding of those moments of grace that God placed within and upon my life's journey.

When understood and appreciated, *grace* lends a moment of peace within the fray of life. A moment outside of time as simple as a smile, an embrace, a caring, a sensation, that assures the person that everything will be all right because God knows us intimately since He created us and loves us more than we will ever understand in this lifetime. This love is beyond measure and amazingly unearned. Those who experience God's grace are flabbergasted that it happened but grateful that it did. And, if they choose to live and to speak about it, their sharing will cause others to learn about and anticipate these possible heavenly gifts in their own lives.

God graces people with talents and then positions them to use these talents effectively. God graces people with inner wisdom to guide and counsel others. God positions (graces) people for service that can aide the plight of others through their intervention. Questions such as "Why am I here?" "What do I have to offer?" "How can I be of service?" are all questions that can only be understood and answered through *grace*. "Be still and know that I am God," is a directive that we need to remind ourselves to follow in belief. "Behold, I make all things new," is also an assurance that God knows what we need and promises to address our longings and needs because He is omnipotent.

A person's eyes have to be open—maybe become wide open—to recognize *grace* when it enters our lives. Believing is seeing in this case. We can often see *grace* operating in another's life when they seem at peace and capable of handling stress. By remaining open to God's hand leading them, they then become the recipients of God's grace most often. People often refer to these types of people as "comfortable in their own skin." Their lives, their bodies, and their spirits seem to fit together in a unified whole.

John O'Donohue states that we are a body inside of a spirit and not a spirit inside of a body. I like this distinction because our bodies are only here for a time, but our spirits are eternal. When we read scripture, it is the spirits of the people that live on as their stories are being told, not their physical bodies. Stories from the Old and New Testaments refine these ideas as a person reads how God's grace entered into a person's life and placed them on a path that they did not predict or foresee for themselves. The Blessed Mother, the Apostles, the Saints, Adam and Eve, Moses, Noah, King David, the Prophets, John the Baptist, and countless others all "channeled" God's grace in order to become their higher selves. Our parents, our families, our ancestors, and our descendants all factor into the continuum of life that can also be referred to as the communion of saints. Our heritage and our legacy can all be viewed within the circle of life that has been and will be continually impacted by God's saving grace.

In the end, knowing that God made us, God loves us, God directs us, God heals us, and God saves us, is part and parcel to the acceptance of God's grace influencing and interacting in our lives. Looking back, it can be seen in the evidence of others' lives well lived that we can learn about through association and through reading. Looking forward, we can anticipate

God's hand in future events in our worldview and our participation in working to make the world a better place in which to live. As good parents protect their young, God too protects His children by bestowing grace in both moments of necessity and in moments of "just because." Like any parent, God enjoys giving whether the recipients are worthy or not. Hopefully, these spontaneous gifts that are not earned or even deserved will inspire us to do likewise in a world in dire need of goodness, graces, gift-giving, and generous responses to the least deserving—which in most circumstances is all of us.

"Pray, and let God worry."
—MARTIN LUTHER

"It is the prayer of faith that moves the hand of God."
—ANGUS BUCHAN

"God does nothing but by prayer, and everything with it."
—JOHN WESLEY

Story Time

Question: How do you acknowledge gratitude in your own life?

Answer: Worry less, praise more. Gratitude opens our hearts and doors to the better things of life. It focuses our minds on the positive and off the negative. It allows for thoughts to flow and for everyone to become a good finder rather than a naysayer. It enables us to enjoy the moment and to prosper from a positive outlook.

Complaining, which is the opposite of gratitude, plugs our imagination and stifles our creative thought processes. It makes people avoid us because of the contagion of negative thought, and causes uneasiness inside of our spirit. Gratitude is the cure, the antidote, the healthy choice!

Do It Now!

Begin right here, right now by doing the activities below.

1. Go the extra mile by being grateful for the life you are given no matter what circumstances you find yourself in. Go deeper until you can find ten things to be grateful for today, right now. Write these down in your journal.

2. What does gratitude look like? Gather images of gratitude and make a collage. When you get gratitude right, your world becomes right.

3. How does gratitude say "thank you?" List ten sentences you can speak to someone expressing your gratitude for things he or she did to bring joy into your life. Now, say these to them and mark DELIVERED.

4. Express gratitude to Nature. Walk outdoors and consider the marvels Nature provides for us daily.

Trees, grass, air, sun, moon, stars, weather—everything. What brings you joy and gratitude?

5. Fall asleep tonight with a litany of gratitude on your life and your prayer in your heart.

Do small things with great love.
—Mother Teresa

Chapter 12

The Alchemy
of Prosperity

*The river is the brain. The flowing force is the
power of thought. The failure side of the stream is
negative thought; the success side is positive thought.*
—NAPOLEON HILL

*The principle by which an idea germinates and grows and
becomes a habit has been designated as cosmic habiforce.*
—NAPOLEON HILL

There is magic in the Universe and because you are a
part and not apart from it, the magic is inside you as
well. Each and every one of us operates under the natural laws of the Universe. These laws are called Cosmic
Habitforce and Infinite Intelligence is behind this plan.

In explanation, Dr. Hill states:

Cosmic habitforce pertains to the entire universe,
and is the law by which the equilibrium of the universe is maintained through established patterns,
or habits. It is the law which forces every living

creature, and every particle of matter, to come under the dominating influence of its environment, including the physical habits and thought habits of mankind.

Ours is a constantly evolving Universe and change is the constant. By embracing change we align ourselves with the process and establish a footing that supports us when we cultivate and engage positive habits and forfeit negative habits. This distillation process of the ego takes a great deal of effort and may be likened to the Alchemy of the Soul, Self, Spirit or whatever name you give to your inner knowing. As the principles of Going the Extra Mile, Definiteness of Purpose, Applied Faith, Personal Initiative, Persistence, Enthusiasm, Self-Discipline, and Mastermind Alliance are cultivated, so too we cultivate and grow our own personal power and energy. We transition from a worthless base or lead personality to one that is golden and priceless. Our value is increased when we focus on positive ideas and remove negative thinking from our thoughts. As we trim, cultivate and polish our inner beings, we begin to shine like the sun and banish personal darkness.

All this talk is metaphorical and resembles the nuances used in poetic writings, but as night follows the day it is true! What you imagine or see yourself becoming you become, but it takes consistent, positive, daily action to bring about this transformation. If and when you do the personal work, the results will follow! When you conceive an idea, and believe in it wholly, you begin to achieve the results because you have conditioned your subconscious mind to do so. What you think about, you bring about every time. Be ready and watchful in your life, because change is about to happen.

As we all know, change can happen overnight. It can also be overwhelming. Often, it takes a person by surprise and literally causes uncomfortable feelings that can also be associated with fear. It is helpful to note that change, fear, and death and dying have several things in common. In order to get a better grip on the hazards that change can pose in someone's altered lifestyle, it is a good idea to look at change from multiple perspectives.

First, in order for growth to occur, change has to happen. The saying "When you're green you grow, when you're ripe you rot" causes us to ponder why change is necessary. Like the yin and yang symbol, change can present both crisis and opportunity. One's attitude can and does determine what comes afterwards.

In his classic book, *Man's Search for Meaning*, Viktor Frankle states that ultimately the only thing man can control is his attitude. Given even the worst of times, one's attitude toward the circumstances is where the future outcome is held. Looking to the possibilities for good rather than the potential for bad, is future oriented and not living in the past. In facing the sunshine, shadows can and do fall behind us.

Second, change is a process not a singular event. The evolution of our species is a history of change and adaptation. By choosing to adapt, a potential future is envisioned. Failure to adapt brings about certain negative outcomes including demise. It has been said that sometimes it is necessary to let the patient die in order to bring about the restorative effects that the death has brought.

In truth, the process of death and dying is much like the process of change. Elizabeth Kubler Ross wrote about the stages of death and dying that include: denial, anger, bargaining, depression, and acceptance. If we think about it, change can and does follow the same pattern.

Joan Chittister writes:

Life without change, we know is dead or deadening. But, never doubt it, change itself can be seen as deadly, too.

Change takes life and tosses it upside down. What was, much as we may have wanted it gone, is no more. Which may be fine at one level, but at another we also know that with this loss goes the loss of everything good that went with it. The familiar, with all its comforts and regularity, disappears. We are left in a maze in the dark to find our ways through to a new life, new relationships, a life without maps and charts to guide us.

So, as we recognize the stages and realize that change is a process, it is reassuring to note that after depression comes acceptance. Once our new situation is accepted, we realize that the scripture passage, "Behold I make all things new," is our invitation to begin again and embrace whatever possibilities life has to offer.

Third, fear is a very real stumbling block in the change process. As Dr. Hill states, things we fear may include the following: Fear of Poverty; Fear of Criticism; Fear of Ill Health; Fear of Loss of Love; Fear of Loss of Liberty/Freedom; Fear of Old Age and Fear of Death. These identified fears can hold us captive and freeze us in our steps toward a new life. Only if we have faith in and trust the process can there be a breakthrough to meaningful change.

This quote by Harriet Tubman captures the fear in risk taking. "If you hear the dogs, keep going. If you see the torches in the woods, keep going. If there's shouting after you, keep going. Don't ever stop. Keep going. If you want the taste of freedom, keep going."

In Margaret Silf's book, *The Other Side of Chaos*, she states that it is time to acknowledge the transition or the "mess" we are living and respond with a "Yes" regarding change in order to bring about what God dreams for us. As our Father, God dreams the very best future for each of us, as we would for our own children. He has loved us into existence, and wants what is best for us as any parent would. In reaching for higher and more benevolent practices as humanity, Silf states that a behavioral evolution can already be seen today in the world by noticing the following:

- In the generosity of spirit with which so many people respond when other people, or indeed other creatures suffer disaster
- In the growing realization that this Earth is a living organism, of which we are an interdependent part and that we have no right to exploit
- In the increasing understanding that unbridled consumerism is not making us more human but is actually tending to dehumanize us, especially when it happens at the expense of our brothers and sisters in lands where poverty is the norm
- In the growing distrust of, and opposition to, military solutions to solve disputes and the demand for more mature solutions to be sought to resolve conflict
- In the escalating search for spiritual meaning in our lives, often expressing itself beyond the boundaries of organized religion
- In the realization that our right brain capabilities of intuition and creativity need to balance our overdeveloped left-brain skills of logic and organization
- In the growing distrust of hierarchy in favor of consensus and co-accountability
- In the growing understanding that our future will depend on cooperation rather than on competition

In considering the above, note that the characteristic acts toward a greater humanity are in accord with Napoleon Hill's teachings. It is no accident that by studying the Science of Success Philosophy of Personal Achievement we are able and encouraged to make the world a better place for each of us and thereby for all of us.

So, what have we learned? It appears that change is a fearsome personal walk that occurs in stages that correspond to the death and dying process. Let's ask ourselves with the above in mind, "Who would want to go through that?" Well, the only answer is that each and every one of us will go through change either gracefully, or kicking and screaming, but we all will go through it sooner or later. If we can bear in mind that it is our attitude in the end that makes the difference in accepting whatever life brings, then we are more open to positive outcomes. Life involves change, change involves risks, and risks taken can and do transport us to a new and hopefully better life.

Thoughtfully, consider "The Guest House" by Jalal Al-Din Rumi. It is a clear challenge to live the life each of us is given.

> *This being human is a guest house.*
> *Every morning a new arrival.*
>
> *A joy, a depression, a meanness,*
> *Some momentary awareness comes*
> *As an unexpected visitor.*

Welcome and entertain them all
Even if they're a crowd of sorrows,
Who violently sweep your house
Empty of its furniture.
Still treat each guest honourably,
He may be clearing you out
For some new delight.

The dark thought. The shame, the malice,
Meet them at the door laughing,
And invite them in.

Be grateful for whoever comes,
Because each has been sent
As a guide from beyond.

- We control our attitudes in life. There are two choices: a positive mental attitude or a negative mental attitude.
- By beginning right where we are in the here and now, we can jumpstart the process of learning this success philosophy by Going the Extra Mile.
- When positive thoughts are cultivated and acted upon, we change ourselves, others and our environment as well.
- By Going the Extra Mile for ourselves and others we instantly see the results of our doing and condition ourselves for doing more of the same.
- The heaviness of living lifts like fog in morning sunlight when we focus on the good we can do rather than worrying about the bad in our lives.

- Doorways are opened that invite more study as success is experienced by first Going the Extra Mile.
- What we do for others in a spirit of harmony begins to be done for us with the same spirit.
- By thinking and doing, we can make it so.
- Little things DO mean a lot, and each little thing contributes to creating habits in our thought patterns and action patterns that all add up to a spiritual and physical change within us.
- Overnight successes do not happen. Saints are not born saints. Status is earned that is meaningful. Follow in the footsteps of the giants you admire. Honor them by emulating their practices. If done in this manner you won't be far behind them.

The above advice is good only if we remember to open the door and welcome the future! You cannot linger in the threshold. You must cross over into the life you imagine for yourself. Now is the time to take that first step that leads to Going the Extra Mile. Safe journey!

Story Time

Question: Is there a downside to change and to Going the Extra Mile?

Answer: Like all things in life, too much of a good thing can be overwhelming. Adjusting to change can be a slow process. In life there are stages for many things that are not simply as easily done as changing clothes. Quick change can be overwhelming and counterproductive. Life works better generally when we ease into a process rather than force it to happen. Take for example the grief that is experienced due to the loss of a loved one. Change has occurred but those left behind may not be ready for a quick change. It can take months and even years for the grieving person to resume living. Friends who go the extra mile may believe that a quick fix can be found in a trip, a dinner, a visit, a new location, etc., but until someone experiences grief, the best thing to do is to be available for help when the person requests it. I have a good friend whose husband just died. She tells me people call and want to go out to dinner, but she says that she is just not ready for it yet. But, she does enjoy when someone cleans the snow off of her car or plows the driveway. In Going the Extra Mile in these circumstances, the best route for the giver is to find a need and fill it. Maybe the best thing to do is simply to ask, "What can I do to help?" The person's response may surprise you, but that is exactly what needs to be done.

Do It Now!

Begin right here, right now, by doing the activities below.

1. How has Going the Extra Mile daily caused you to change both your perspective and outcome in today's world?

2. What have you done differently that has contributed to your positive change? What can you continue to do in order to make your change a permanent habit?

3. By "habitizing" your actions, how do you gain control of your goals and Definite Major Purpose?

4. How can you use your knowledge of the change process to better gauge your journey towards the success that you desire in life?

5. Before falling asleep, express gratitude once again for all good things today has brought to you and you have given to others.

6. Close the evening with your personal prayer.

Hang on to your hat. Hang on to your hope.
And wind the clock, for tomorrow is another day.
—E.B. WHITE

Chapter 13

The Plus Factor

*Cosmic habitforce will take over this habit of Going the
Extra Mile and make it a fixation which will be of untold
benefit to you. You'll find yourself doing it automatically,
just for the good feeling it gives you deep down inside.*
—NAPOLEON HILL

*Self-discipline is the tool with which man may harness and
direct his inborn emotions in the direction of his choice.*
—NAPOLEON HILL

Through repetition and practice, things we do daily
evolve into habits that become our second nature.
Unfortunately, positive deeds and negative deeds
work in the same way. Over time, one or the other
can easily become ingrained in our subconscious
minds. Caution needs to be exerted here in order for
only positive habits to become fixed in our nature.
Only the things that we want to see manifested in
our lives need to be given our attention.

Consider the following list of negative habits and
ask yourself if you have permitted some of them to
take up residence in your mind.

Negative Habits:
- Poverty
- Drifting without aim or purpose
- Imaginary illness
- Irritability of mental attitude
- Laziness
- The will to injure others
- Envy
- Jealousy
- Greed
- Dishonesty
- Vanity
- Arrogance
- Cynicism
- Sadism

If you have acquired some of these negative habits over time, the antidote is to remove them through the acquisition of the positive habits listed below.

Positive Habits:
- Definiteness of purpose
- Enthusiasm
- Faith
- Self-discipline
- Personal initiative
- Going the extra mile

Going the extra mile once again appears on the short list of ways to develop positive habits. Dr. Hill states: "The way to make this habit a fixation is to start right now to do something for which you do not expect to be paid directly."

Again, the directive is simple and concrete. By beginning at the onset of your study of the Philosophy of Success with Going the Extra Mile, you will put the Universe in your debt and sooner or later you will be duly rewarded.

Cosmic Habitforce is said to be the comptroller of the Universe and what works for one person must therefore work for all. This universal plan is demonstrated in the orderliness of the world. The natural media of creation supplies one and the same opportunity to everyone because we are not separate from the Universal Plan, but a part of it. Therefore, we are under its jurisdiction like it or not.

It only makes sense to utilize this Universal Plan in attaining our desired outcome in life. This is begun by establishing a definite major purpose followed by a definite plan for its attainment.

Poet Dylan Thomas describes Cosmic Habitforce as "The force that through the green fuse drives the flower." It is a beautiful image if you look at a plant about to blossom. The anticipation and wonder are captured for the observer as the bud forces itself up through the plant.

Later in the poem he states that this same force drives his red blood through his veins, or allows it to dry up. Things both good and bad, or positive and negative, occur because of Cosmic Habitforce. The reality is that we, as participants and observers of the Natural Laws of the Universe, label things due to our perspective. Cosmic Habitforce just *is*—neither good nor bad, but our thinking makes it so.

In "Pied Beauty," Gerard Manley Hopkins writes extensively about things that are dappled or spotted such as cows and trout. He lists many things that have this characteristic. Concluding, he acknowledges all these things as gifts from God, and simply ends with the words "Praise him."

> Glory be to God for dappled things —
>   For skies of couple-colour as a brinded cow;
>   For rose-moles all in stipple upon trout that swim;
>   Fresh-firecoal chestnut-falls; finches' wings;
>   Landscape plotted and pieced—fold, fallow, and plough;
>   And all trades, their gear and tackle and trim.
>
> All things counter, original, spare, strange;
>   Whatever is fickle, freckled (who knows how?)
>   With swift, slow; sweet, sour; adazzle, dim;
>   He fathers-forth whose beauty is past change:
>   Praise him.

The two poems are different, yet both speak to the nature of Cosmic Habitforce. Dylan Thomas considers both sides of the effect the laws of nature have upon each and every one of us, while Hopkins focuses only on the beauty. We can do either or both, but whatever way we look at the world we are born into, acknowledgment must be made that it is our responsibility to control our thoughts and our mental attitude and no one else's.

In conclusion, Dr. Hill states:

> It seems an appropriate summary for this lesson to state that the nucleus of this entire philosophy of individual achievement lies in cosmic habitforce.

Here is the process for aligning with Cosmic Habitforce as defined by Dr. Hill:

> Control your mental attitude, keep it positive by exercising self-discipline, and thus prepare the mental soil in which any worthwhile plan, purpose or desire may be planted by repeated, intense impression, with the assurance that it will germinate, grow and find expression ultimately in its material equivalent, through whatever means are at hand.

Notice too that Dr. Hill uses imagery. He compares the process of cultivating your definite major purpose to planting a seed of thought. Remember, what we think about we bring about. Each of us growing our own victory garden one plant at a time.

Story Time

Question: How has Cosmic Habitforce played a significant role in my life?

Answer: Cosmic Habitforce has a way of bringing things into our lives when we least expect them. Perhaps a new acquaintance, an unexpected trip, a gift, an awareness, a birth, a death, an illness, and anything additional you can imagine. A quotation from Thomas Kempis reads: "For man proposes, but God disposes; neither is the way of man in his own hands." Try as we might, things do not often turn out as we planned. Perhaps, this is God's way of saying "Yes" or "No."

I recall in my life struggling to complete many things and the struggle made it seem as if I were going against the tide. Other times, things came easily and without the struggle. Those things seemed to put me on a positive path for my life, while the things I struggled with caused me continual upset and stress.

I remember my University mentor, Dr. Sefler, advising me to leave a position in school administration because as he stated: "they do not appreciate your gifts." This occurred after a Magic Performance he gave to the primary and middle school children and found that he could not make them laugh. Out loud, he wondered why this happened. At the time, I wanted to do more for the students and the school, but I heeded his advice and took another position in an adjacent school community more to my liking.

After two more positions, I was asked to apply for the position of Director of the Napoleon Hill World Learning Center located on the campus of Purdue Calumet. Had I not been open to transitioning in employment, I would never have accepted the position that I spent seventeen years enjoying. Funny how Cosmic Habitforce works. It reminds me of a Christian Song, "When Jesus say yes, nobody can say no."

Do It Now!

Begin right here, right now, by doing the activities below.

1. Reread the process for aligning with Cosmic Habitforce above. Detail how you are following the bullet points and receiving the benefits as of today.

2. Consider a time when Cosmic Habitforce has changed the course of your life. What did you learn from the experience?

3. How can you help someone going through this process by Going the Extra Mile?

4. Anticipate what can come next by your ongoing study of Dr. Hill's Philosophy of Success. If one principle—Going the Extra Mile—has contributed to your well-being, consider what the other sixteen could do.

5. Begin now to assemble your roadmap to success by journeying along the proven success path of

countless individuals who have studied this philosophy. Step one is complete. Apply it daily.

6. Now, express gratitude for the knowledge you have been given and decide, here and now, to apply it for your good and the good of mankind in order to make a positive difference for yourself and others.

Stay the Course!

Boldness has genius, power, and magic in it.
—Johann Wolfgang von Goethe

About the Author

Judith A. Williamson is a retired teacher and school administrator living in Valparaiso, Indiana and Columbia, Kentucky. For seventeen years she served as the Educational Director for the Napoleon Hill Foundation located at Purdue Calumet. In this position, she wrote extensive materials and conducted training seminars around the world on the topic of Keys to Success. Previously, she taught locally and worked in administration at area high schools as principal and assistant principal. For four years she worked as the Coordinator of Development for the Diocese of Gary working primarily with the Catholic Services Appeal. Her passions are travel, reading and writing, and animals. She has one dog, Lena, twenty cats, and one lovebird. She has visited Russia, China, Ireland, and Egypt. In November, 2019 she headed to Uganda with a mission group from Kentucky. Recently, she worked with the migrants in El Paso and San Antonio coordinated by Sr. Edith PHJC, and Sr. Connie PHJC. In becoming an Associate for the Poor Handmaids of Jesus Christ, she hopes to contribute more by understanding and applying the charisms of Saint Katharina Kasper in her own life and in helping others.

She has two children, Timothy and Cathleen. Tim lives in Alexandria, VA and has four children; three boys and a girl. Cathleen lives in St. Louis, MO., and, following in her mother's footsteps, has a dog, Beau, and three cats, but no birds yet.